Discovering Royal Doulton

King Charles I (HN3459, Charles Noke and Harry Tittensor, 1992). Produced in a limited edition of 350 to commemorate the 350th anniversary of the English Civil War in 1642.

Discovering
Royal Doulton

MICHAEL DOULTON
In association with
VINNY LEE

SWAN·HILL
PRESS

Acknowledgements

I am indebted to many colleagues at Royal Doulton for their help and encouragement in the preparation of this book.

I am grateful to Chairman, Stuart Lyons, and to Ann Linscott and other colleagues who have supported the project and, in particular, to Valerie Baynton and Mary Moorcroft for their proof-reading, photograph preparation and selection and general help. Also to Katherine Ellis and Ian Howe who have advised over content and to Anita Fitchett who provided much administrative support.

Many personnel at Royal Doulton factories have been consulted and freely given their time. I would like to thank Amanda Dickson and her Design team; William Whitehead and all Production departments; and Chris Pearson and the Marketing team.

Photography was undertaken by Northern Counties Photography, and I wish to thank Gerald Wells for his enthusiasm and advice.

Last, but not least, this project could not have been completed without the continued help, patience and encouragement of my wife, Pruna.

First published in the UK in 1993
by Swan Hill Press an imprint of Airlife Publishing Ltd.

British Library Cataloguing in Publication Data
A catalogue record for this book
is available from the British Library

ISBN 1 85310 343 8

Printed by Kyodo Printing Co. (S'pore) Pte Ltd., Singapore.

Swan Hill Press
an imprint of Airlife Publishing Ltd.
101 Longden Road, Shrewsbury SY3 9EB

Contents

Henley (HN3367, Valerie Annand, 1993). The first model in the British Sporting Heritage Series produced in a limited edition of 5,000.

Preface

Michael Doulton

Allow me to introduce myself. I am Michael Doulton, the sixth generation of the Doulton family to be involved in the internationally renowned Royal Doulton Company. Since 1976 my role within the Company has been that of travelling ambassador, and with the launch of the Royal Doulton International Collectors Club in 1980 I became its Honorary President. During my trips around Great Britain, Canada, America, Australia and other parts of the world I have met many people, some first-time purchasers of our china, others well-established collectors. My work also involves appearing on television, giving newspaper interviews and taking part in radio programmes both at home and abroad. I host in store promotions, signings and special events on behalf of Royal Doulton. Collectors' fairs and specialist events for the trade and antique collectors also feature in my diary.

Through these diverse visits, events and meetings with customers and retailers I build up a first-hand view of the marketplace. I can see for myself how well a new figure, Character Jug or another product is received. Prospective purchasers often tell me what they are looking for in a piece and their reasons for choosing one item rather than another, or if they have a gap in their collection that we might be able to fill. All this information is carefully noted and put into my reports. The findings are then discussed with our marketing and sales teams as well as design and production departments.

Over the years, people have asked me numerous questions concerning the Company and its products. Some have been interested in the history of Royal Doulton and its various manufacturing techniques. Others have enquired about collecting – how to display and care for their collection or where to buy items they want to complete their own displays. Although I do my best to furnish them with a reply, my time is often limited and in the confines of a bustling china shop it is difficult to go into detail. So, to answer many of those queries in a fuller and more satisfactory way, I have prepared this book.

Ideally, every Royal Doulton purchaser should visit and tour our factories in Stoke-on-Trent to see the skills and talents of our personnel at work. As this is not possible for

Group of Pretty Lady figures, introduced in 1990. Left to right: My Best Friend (HN3011, Peter Gee); Alexandra (HN3286, Douglas Tootle); Elizabeth (HN2465, John Bromley); Morning Breeze (HN3313, Peter Gee).

everyone, I will explain the most important techniques used in creating some of our ranges. These include our famous sculpted figures and Character Jugs as well as tablewares and the specialist advertising merchandise. I feel that a little knowledge of the making of a figure will add to your appreciation and enjoyment of the intrinsic beauty of a piece. Although our Pretty Ladies are currently the most popular collectable items, few people realise just how much is involved in the making of the china figures displayed in their homes.

I will also touch on the area of collecting, an increasingly popular pastime and one to which I contribute with my own specially produced 'Michael Doulton' figure – only available during my personal appearances in stores. Royal Doulton is collected by many people, each specialising in their own particular area, whether it be figures or plates, new or old. The Royal Doulton International Collectors Club has over 25,000 members around the world, and more join each year.

It is possible to see fine displays of Royal Doulton pieces in many museums. A magnificent 50-foot ceramic frieze, 'Pottery through the Ages', which once decorated the façade of the Royal Doulton headquarters in Lambeth, south London, now rests above the main staircase leading to the ceramics exhibits in the Victoria and Albert Museum, London. Modelled by the distinguished sculptor Gilbert Bayes, this colourful frieze was made in Doulton's polychrome stoneware, a revolutionary durable finish suitable for architectural work, which first attracted Bayes to the Company. The 'ages' of pottery shown in the frieze cover eight distinct periods and locations – Assyria, Persia, Crete, Greece, Phoenicia, Rome, the Orient and Renaissance Italy.

Most of the factory buildings at Lambeth were demolished in 1978 but the frieze was saved by a team of enthusiasts and painstakingly restored over several years at the Ironbridge Gorge Museum, Shropshire. A smaller panel, originally sited on the north face of the Lambeth building, and still at this museum, shows the arrival of the Dutch Delft potters at Lambeth.

The Powerhouse Museum in Sydney, Australia has a particularly fine range of Royal Doulton because it is based on the personal collection of one of the Company's most celebrated art directors, John Slater. Royal Doulton can also

Detail from the 50-foot relief panel in coloured stoneware of 'Pottery Through the Ages', by Gilbert Bayes. Now on display in the Victoria and Albert Museum, London.

be found in smaller museums such as the British Bottle Museum at Elsecar, Barnsley in Yorkshire, England which has a substantial display of Royal Doulton's early drink dispensers and bottles.

My place in the Doulton family tree is a frequent source of interest to the people I meet, and as I am introducing myself in this preface it seems an appropriate place to explain briefly the Doulton hierarchy and succession. The founder of the Company – my great, great, great grandfather — was John Doulton (1793–1873). He trained as a potter in south London at the Fulham Pottery, before joining a small business owned by a widow named Martha Jones. Her only son got into trouble with the law and had to leave the country quickly. He was not heard of again during the widow's lifetime. Left without an heir, the widow invited John Doulton and another manager in the pottery to become her business partners. After much consultation with his family John invested their life savings of £100 in the small firm.

At this time the Company, known as Doulton and Watts, was based on the south bank of the River Thames and produced mostly utilitarian saltglaze and stoneware ceramics, stone jars, bottles and flasks. Five of John's sons later joined their father in the business. But it was the second son, Henry, who ignored possible careers in politics or the church to take his place in the pottery. Henry became a master potter, giving him first-hand knowledge of the business, from the production stages through to management. His entrepreneurial and pioneering spirit led to the expansion and diversification of the Company. In the 1840s he established the world's first factory for making stoneware drainpipes – an important contribution at that time of social reform when legislation was being passed for improvements in health care, sanitary conditions and the provision of piped water.

In 1849 Henry met and married a Miss Sarah Kennaby. On their honeymoon in the Lake District they met the poet William Wordsworth, whom Henry greatly admired. The newly-wed Mr and Mrs Doulton settled at 7 Stockwell Villas, South Lambeth Road, close to the pottery.

In the early 1870s, alongside the thriving pipe business, Henry opened an art studio and set out to encourage and employ talented artists, many of whom came from the neighbouring Lambeth Art College. Seven years later he bought a factory at Burslem in Stoke-on-Trent and, to the annoyance of the established potters in the 'mother town' of the Potteries, the Londoner moved into their domain and in 1884 began to make fine bone china.

In the following year Henry was honoured for his achievements, receiving the Albert Medal of the Society of Arts. Only one Albert Medal was awarded each year and previous recipients included the poet Alfred, Lord Tennyson and Sir Rowland Hill for his many achievements but, in particular, for his creation of the penny postage system. This prestigious award was given to Henry for his 'encouragement in the production of artistic pottery'. However Henry Doulton received his greatest honour in 1887 when Queen Victoria awarded him a knighthood – the first potter ever to be distinguished in this way. Sir Henry died in 1897 leaving behind a Company that had grown and diversified and become established as one of the leaders in its field.

Sir Henry's son, Henry Lewis Doulton (1853–1930), became a partner in 1881. Four years after his father's death, he received, on behalf of the Company, the Royal Warrant of King Edward Vll. The monarch also granted permission to add the word 'Royal' to the Doulton name, a great and rare honour. In his role as Chairman and managing director Henry Lewis guided the Company through the difficult recession and war periods of 1900 to 1920. Henry Lewis Doulton was particularly interested in experimental glazes such as Rouge Flambé, Sung and Chang, and encouraged their development. Rouge Flambé is a glaze still unique to Royal Doulton today; it is produced to the same secret formula known only to three or four people in the Company.

John Doulton, 1793-1873.

Sir Henry Doulton, 1820-1897, from a drawing by Frederick Sandys.

Royal Doulton, Nile Street, Burslem, Stoke-on-Trent.

The Albert Medal of the 'Society of Arts' was awarded to Henry Doulton in 1885 and was presented to him on 21 December by the Prince of Wales (later Edward VII) at the Lambeth factory.

Ronald Duneau Doulton (1852–1929), a cousin of Henry Lewis Doulton and grandson of the founder John, was involved in the management and administration and became one of the first directors of Doulton and Co in 1899. Next in line was Lewis John Eric Hooper (1879-1955), son of Henry Lewis's sister Lily and consequently John's great grandson. Eric, as he was known, joined Royal Doulton in 1902 at 23 years of age. He had an honours degree in Law from Oxford and had been called to the Bar, but left the legal profession to follow in the family firm. Eric is said to have had many of his grandfather Henry's characteristics including an amazing and retentive memory. Under Eric's guidance much scientific research into the physical and chemical behaviour of ceramic materials was carried out and from the results new technology was developed and installed.

Orrok Sherwood Doulton (1916-77), my father and Eric's nephew, joined the Company in 1935 becoming a director in 1953. His interests included motorcycle racing, regarded as a rather risqué sport at the time, but one in which he successfully competed. He became the first Englishman to win the Belgian Grand Prix. The story goes that he told his mother he was going to Belgium for the weekend with friends. That Sunday morning as she read the front page of the newspaper, she was greeted by a headline telling her that her son had become a motorcycling champion!

During my father's directorship Royal Doulton won the Queen's Award for Industry twice; in 1966 for Technological Innovation, for the development of English Translucent China (now known as fine china), the first Company in the ceramic industry to achieve such an award; and in 1970 for Outstanding Export Performance. Father had the honour of meeting The Queen and on several occasions Prince Philip, The Duke of Edinburgh.

I remember as a child, our father taking my only brother Mark and me to the Lambeth works in south London. The Company worked on Saturdays in those days, so it was our weekend treat to be allowed to accompany him – although I am sure we must have been a nuisance. I can still recall the

salty atmosphere there, salty because the saltglaze pots were literally covered with salt and the insides of the kilns were shiny and smooth like glass from the residue of the salt being burnt onto the walls. To an eight-year-old it was a magical place, the heat of the vast kilns like ogre's caves, with leather-aproned men hauling great trollies of pottery in and out of the kilns, sweat running down their faces from the heat. But the art studios were the highlight of any visit and there we were allowed to model clay into what were undoubtedly useless shapes. I still have a couple of dreadful masks I made and painted, but at the time the thrill of making something and having it fired was part of the magic.

This early introduction to the manufacture of pottery encouraged my interest in the Company, and it would have been difficult for me not to have become involved in the business. At preparatory school I remember a boy coming up and telling me that he had just seen my surname in the WC – our ceramic wares turn up in all sorts of unexpected places! As a teenager I occasionally visited the Stoke-on-Trent factory but my early impressions and memories are all from the Lambeth business. As I was growing up I had a hankering at the back of my mind to work for Royal Doulton. My brother Mark joined the Company quite soon after he left school and had to do a few years learning the business by working his way round the factory, getting to know each process and department. Mark then worked for Royal Doulton for a number of years on the management side but also owned a couple of china shops selling Royal Doulton china. When Mark gave up his job within the Company he concentrated on running his shops. Unfortunately he died in February 1991.

Midinette (HN2090, Leslie Harradine, 1952-1965).

Taking Things Easy (HN2677, Mary Nicoll, 1975-1987).

a minimum. These and numerous other advances have allowed us to develop our skills in other areas such as hand painting. The quality and diversity of finishes have improved greatly in the last ten years. I feel that Royal Doulton is a Company that combines art and industry, a Company where traditional craftsmanship works alongside new technology.

As I travel the world visiting our various retail outlets I am always reminded that Royal Doulton's present success is based on our past record. Our future sales depend on the quality and finesse of the last piece we made, so standards must always be kept high. What we make today may be the antiques and collectables of the future.

As for the next generation of Doultons, my late brother's son Sherwood, named after my father, is still at school and hopes to join the R.A.F. Through my marriage, in 1987, to Pruna I have two step-daughters, Annabelle and Sacha Barraclough. Their father, Anthony Barraclough, was a great friend of mine and we shared an apartment in Point Piper in Sydney, Australia in the 1960s. Anthony returned to England a couple of months before me to marry Pruna. On my return to England I met Pruna and I was made god-father to their first child Annabelle. Sadly Anthony died not long after the birth of his second daughter Sacha. Sometime later I met Pruna again and we married; now my god-daughter Annabelle and her sister Sacha both live with us in our south London home.

I eventually joined Royal Doulton in 1970 having first worked in London as a stockbroker and then spent several years in Australia. Whilst working Down Under I took six months' holiday to drive around the country and accidentally steered my four-wheel-drive off a small cliff in northern Queensland. I had to spend a month sleeping rough waiting for a spare back axle, and because I needed some money I joined forces with a game hunter to shoot crocodiles. After this adventure I returned to Sydney and was involved in retail research and development with the Grace Brothers Company. The latter experience still stands me in good stead today as I proudly travel the world visiting shops displaying the quality products that Royal Doulton create and manufacture.

When I first joined the Company I was sent to Stoke-on-Trent where I lived and worked for six weeks. I was not allowed to use my own name when I worked in the factory, so I was given a fictitious cover. I'm not sure whether the management thought I might get preferential treatment or whether they thought the staff might think I was spying on them. I was involved in all aspects of production and found that I was more suited to making than painting. I can remember my days in the decorating department and being set the task of painting a figure called 'Taking Things Easy' (HN2677) – which my workmates thought was a bit of a joke. But I found it far from easy to paint and took three times as long as anyone else. My lasting memories of those introductory weeks at Stoke are of the camaraderie of my workmates and the pride they had in their work.

To my mind Royal Doulton still follows in the established tradition of the Company, keeping ahead of the current market and trends. We now have machines to help make such items as plates, which were extremely labour intensive and very monotonous to produce. Our high-tech kilns fire the ware in hours rather than days and our losses are kept to

Michael Doulton pouring slip into a mould to cast the figure Southern Belle (HN2229).

The girls have both shown great interest in the Doulton family history and the Royal Doulton company. For her 'A' level History of Art dissertation Annabelle concentrated on the early years of Royal Doulton Lambeth Ware 1815 to 1900. This has now been included in the Royal Doulton archives. Sacha is a little too young to be making that sort of choice – although she is a keen collector of Bunnykins ware and has painted her own versions of the 'Old Balloon Seller' and a 'Pretty Lady' figure.

My work for Royal Doulton keeps me very busy and in my time I have been caught up in dramas. Once the plane I was travelling on to Miami was hi-jacked to Cuba. On another occasion, while visiting a store in Queens, New York, I was the subject of a bomb threat. The FBI escorted me back to my hotel and searched my room. Fortunately the threat turned out to be a hoax. In any year I spend about six or seven months working abroad, visiting customers in Canada, the Caribbean, Australia and America. We are currently expanding into new markets in South America and the Far East. The rest of the year is taken up with events at home, visiting our UK outlets, attending Collectors Club events or marketing and planning meetings at Royal Doulton's head office in Stoke-on-Trent. Sometimes my wife Pruna travels with me – otherwise there are times when we wouldn't see each other for weeks at a time. Pruna sometimes attends Collectors Club meetings and shop events. She is also a Royal Doulton collector.

As I live in south London I occasionally find myself in Lambeth, often *en route* to Waterloo Station travelling for

A terracotta panel by George Tinworth showing the interior of the Lambeth Art Studio. Note the cat under Hannah Barlow's chair to the left of the illustration.

Royal Doulton. Although it is nearly forty years since the Company left this original site, there are still memories and signs of its presence. Vauxhall Walk is a quiet, narrow street running parallel to the Albert Embankment and the River Thames. If you half close your eyes you can imagine how it might have been with the horse-drawn vehicles clattering along the cobbled paths, the sooty atmosphere made by the pottery's coal-fired kilns and the heat and clamour of the bustling factory.

As you walk along to Lambeth High Street you pass by Tinworth Street, named after the Company's famous sculptor. When you cross Black Prince Road into Lambeth High Street you cannot fail to notice the magnificent façade of the former Doulton showrooms and studios. It appears like some enchanted castle with its rounded windows and ornate decoration, a unique, decorated jewel amongst the surrounding modern sheet-glass and concrete office blocks. The building now houses a direct mail operation but the panel above the door tells of its previous connections. The panel, by George Tinworth, shows a scene in the pottery studio. To the left is a lady sitting on a stool painting a vase. Beside her is another vase with a lion's head decoration on its side and under her seat is a crouched domestic cat – tell-tale signs that the lady is none other than Hannah Barlow, Doulton's noted animal illustrator. In the centre of the panel is an artist, perhaps Tinworth himself, in a smock-like working coat, holding a vase. The bearded gentlemen to his right study the vessel with great interest. The most prominent of these gentlemen is most likely to be Sir Henry Doulton.

Apart from the panel there are many coloured ceramic tiles and the detail in these is exquisite, even by contemporary standards. Around the windows are column-shaped tiles made to look like bundles of wheat. Each tiny ear and grain of the cereal is shown in relief. On the lower

Michael Doulton at a Collectors Event in Eatons, Canada.

walls of the building, green, blue and yellow floral and geometric tiles provide a border against the buff and red of the fancy terracotta and brick work.

As you reach the end of Lambeth High Street you face the imposing building of Lambeth Palace. When I see the Palace from Lambeth High Street, it reminds me of an indignant letter my forebear, Henry Doulton, received from the Archbishop of Canterbury in the winter of 1872. The Archbishop complained that the fumes, caused by the salt-glaze kilns of the pottery, were entering Lambeth Palace and causing him inconvenience.

In front of the Palace is the church of St Mary at Lambeth, also the Museum of Garden History and burial place of the Tradescants, father and son gardeners in the reign of Charles I, who travelled in Europe and America collecting many flowers, shrubs and trees. In the church you can see two Doulton terracotta panels by George Tinworth. The first, on your right as you come through the door, was erected in 1899 to the memory of John Hernaman, headmaster of the local boys school – perhaps teacher to many of the Doulton staff and workers. Almost opposite is a single panel, originally part of a reredos or three-part screen intended to cover the wall behind the altar. The reredos had been erected by Sir Henry Doulton in 1888 in memory of his wife Sarah who died in that year. The other two panels were destroyed and the single remaining panel, salvaged in 1941, is now displayed in a wooden frame on the church wall.

But let us move from the past to the present and our busy operations in Stoke-on-Trent where the Royal Doulton tradition of combining the best of art and industry not only continues but advances into the future.

Stuart Lyons, CBE, Chief Executive of the Royal Doulton Company.

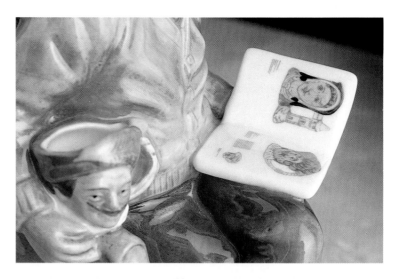

Right: Detail of 'Pride and Joy' (HN2945).

A selection of commissions for the Royal Doulton International Collectors Club. Left to right: Geisha (HN3229, Pauline Parsons, 1989); L'Ambitieuse (HN3359, Valerie Annand, 1991); Top o'the Hill plate (designed by Neil Faulkner, 1985); Old King Cole Character Jug (Harry Fenton, 1990); Columbus Character Jug (Stanley Taylor, 1992); Pride and Joy (HN2945, Robert Tabbenor, 1984).

Chapter 1
COLLECTORS AND COLLECTING

During my travels I talk to people making their first Royal Doulton purchase, as well as to dedicated enthusiasts anxiously awaiting a new plate or figure to add to their existing collections. Whether a new collector or an established one, the common bond of owning a piece of Royal Doulton china, with its unique heritage and international appeal, provides an introduction.

After more than twenty years in the business I am still surprised by the number of themes people find to base their collections on. When I am asked what I think someone should collect, I advise choosing pieces for pleasure rather than for financial gain. Although some collections are undoubtedly valuable, it is just as important there should be visual enjoyment as well.

Many Royal Doulton collections have started with a gift – a decorative wedding present or a birthday present from a grandmother to her grandchild or from a husband to a wife. From just one ornament or Bunnykins mug the urge to collect can be triggered. I know of a gentleman in Florida who was given, as a birthday present, an old saltglaze mug by his wife. He now owns a collection of similar items valued in excess of a quarter of a million dollars.

I regularly meet people during my shop visits who tell me how they started collecting. A young girl was given a Reflections figure by her parents for her eighteenth birthday. She had just had another birthday and with the money she had been given by relations she was buying her second Reflections figure. A man had bought his first Royal Doulton figure for a girlfriend because it had her name. Now, many years later he was buying the girlfriend, now his wife, and their three little girls, figures to commemorate the birth of their third daughter. One lady took me by surprise, when she bought ten examples of Angela (HN3419), my figure of the year in 1992. She asked me to sign them all and while I was scribbling my way through the figures I asked her why she was buying so many of the same model. She replied that her name was Angela and she was giving every member of her family a figure as a memento.

Popular themes for collections include Commemorative wares – any plate, mug or figure with Royal connections or in celebration of an event. Animals are perennially popular and can cover a wide variety of Royal Doulton products from painted plates, figures, Pretty Lady figures with pets and even Character Jugs – there was a fierce-looking British bulldog on the handle of the 1992 Winston Churchill Character Jug of the Year.

Patricia (HN3365, Valerie Annand, Figure of the Year, 1993).

Some collectors choose the work of one modeller or decorator, for example the late Peggy Davies's figures, or the plates designed by Neil Faulkner. To a perceptive eye, the particular style of one modeller can be recognised above another. For keen collectors of Pretty Ladies there are other criteria that may influence their choice. Some collectors do not like figures that have the toe of the shoe peeping from under the skirts and others collect by hair colour, favouring blondes, brunettes or the more rare redhead. Variations occur between figures because each one is decorated by hand by one of a team of artists. Buying a figure is not like buying a picture print that is copied exactly, time after time. Each china figure is individually decorated, a piece of art, bearing the mark and personal touch of its artist.

Particular glazes or shapes may also appeal. For example the strong red and black colouring of Flambé ware (for more

The World is one theme for a collection which can include many aspects of Royal Doulton. Left to right: The Mandarin (HN450, Charles Noke, 1921 to 1938); Refuge, from the Jungle Fantasy Series (Gustavo Novoa, Collectors International plate, 1980); Beefeater Character Jug (Harry Fenton, introduced in 1947); Spanish Flamenco Dancer (HN2831, from the limited edition series Dancers of the World, Peggy Davies, 1977).

detail on this glaze see page 115) is a very specific taste which does not appeal to everyone. Flambé is successfully used to decorate animal and bird shapes as well as figures. Some figures are based on an oriental theme such as the Geisha (HN3229), the Genie (HN2999) and Confucius (HN3314). I have found that this particular type of ware is popular with men, perhaps because the colouring is plainer but dramatic and the shapes and modelling detail of the figures come into their own.

Series Ware, which dates back to 1889, is keenly sought. The designs, based on themes such as the works of Dickens, *The Canterbury Tales*, Rip Van Winkle or Old English Inns, were used to decorate whole ranges of shapes. Teapots, mugs, jugs, biscuit barrels, candlesticks and plates were decorated with motifs on the same theme. For example illustrations of Anne Hathaway's Cottage, Kenilworth Castle and Guy's Cliff Mill formed part of the Shakespeare's Country group and collecting each item in the range is a hobby which is growing in popularity.

Fashion is another idea for a collection. Here the figures illustrate different hair styles popular between 1920 and 1970. Left to right: Cicely (HN1516, Leslie Harradine, 1932-1949); Lynne (HN2329, Peggy Davies, introduced in 1971); Columbine (HN2185, Peggy Davies, 1957-1969); Negligée (HN1219, Leslie Harradine, 1927-1938).

A more recent trend has emerged for gathering what are known as Advertising Wares. Royal Doulton has long had associations with distilleries such as the whisky companies of Dewars, Grants and Haig, for whom special presentation flagons and saltglaze bottles were produced. Commercial gifts and tableware such as inkstands, ashtrays and matchstrikers were also produced for such businesses as the London Electric Wire Co. & Smiths Ltd, and Moët & Chandon. Within the last few years Royal Doulton has created a ceramic turkey for Bernard Matthews' poultry Company and commemorative ware for the Quaker Oats Company's eightieth anniversary. Small, limited editions of these wares are commissioned, sometimes only in a quantity equivalent to the number of staff or directors of the firm concerned, therefore making the pieces rare.

My own collecting habits are quite random. Rather than collect everything in one particular field I tend to gather three or four items on one theme and then change my allegiance and start collecting another style or group. I have a number of beautiful pieces that I have found on my travels and brought home. There are others that I have seen and pondered about and then missed the opportunity to buy, and later regretted the loss bitterly. I have to try to be disciplined about what I collect, otherwise our home would be filled to the doors and my wife and family would have to fit in around the china! The problem is that the Company produces so many wonderful wares that it is hard to restrict the collecting urge.

My mother is still a collector. She seems to concentrate on Pretty Lady figures and animals but she often buys new pieces from Royal Doulton's very latest ranges. My father, as well as being a motorbike enthusiast, was also interested in sailing and his collection was based on a nautical theme. I suppose you could class Bunnykins as my earliest collected range, as it was from Bunnykins china that, as children, we took our first meals.

Collecting can also be a self-educating process. I know people who have started by doing a little initial research and reading into the manufacture or history of a piece, only to find themselves fascinated. They become enthusiasts and carry on to find out more and sometimes become very knowledgeable in their special field. Such people often approach us for further information from our considerable archive collection and reference material in the Sir Henry Doulton Gallery (see page 139). Collectors can consult and use the resources of our historical department by sending a photograph of their Royal Doulton ware and asking us about our findings on such an item.

There is a unique charm about Royal Doulton's wares. The pleasure comes not only from the beauty of the pieces but also in the history and quality of the goods. There are few businesses these days who can claim a continuous family presence in the firm for six generations. In 1979 the Victoria and Albert Museum in London held an exhibition called 'The Doulton Story', which followed the history and development of the Doulton potteries. The Victoria and Albert Museum has a number of Royal Doulton pieces, amongst them a panel entitled 'Instruction' in the quadrangle and the magnificent frieze depicting 'Pottery through the Ages'.

Over the two and a half months of the Victoria and Albert Museum's Doulton exhibition we received numerous requests for more information and discovered that there were hundreds of collectors of the various types of Royal Doulton pottery from the oldest Lambeth Wares of the mid-nineteenth century to the most recent Pretty Ladies and Character Jugs.

In response to the public's enthusiastic questioning and interest we launched the Royal Doulton International Collectors Club in 1980 (see page 141). Our collectors have proved to be a great source not only of ideas but information. A number of dedicated collectors have helped us build-up and develop our own archive information and displays. Following on from what we learned about the trends of collecting we have been able to develop lines to add to popular ranges.

Members of the Royal Doulton International Collectors Club receive a regular magazine, *Gallery*, with news of events around the world. They are also given the opportunity to purchase special offers of figures and other pieces made exclusively for the club. Complimentary tours of the factory are also available, and regular meetings of club members take place in England, Canada, Australia, New Zealand and America. Collectors and smaller clubs in South Africa, Malaysia and many other parts of the world are kept up-to-date with Royal Doulton news, direct from the Stoke-on-Trent office.

The International Collectors Club was originally based in London, but in 1990 it transferred to the Company's headquarters in Stoke-on-Trent. This was done to enable the staff to have easier access to the archives to research queries and to be in closer contact with the latest developments and running of the Company.

Military Heroes as depicted on Character Jugs is a third idea for a collection. Left to right: Winston Churchill (Jug of the Year, 1992, Stanley Taylor); Montgomery of El Alamein (Stanley Taylor, 1992), limited edition of 2,500. Soldier and Airman both by Bill Harper.

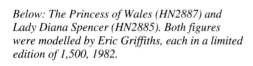

Right: Three Pretty Lady models, Autumn Breezes (HN2131, Leslie Harradine, introduced in 1990); Sara (HN3308, Peggy Davies, introduced in 1981); Elaine (HN3307, Peggy Davies, introduced in 1990).

Below: The Princess of Wales (HN2887) and Lady Diana Spencer (HN2885). Both figures were modelled by Eric Griffiths, each in a limited edition of 1,500, 1982.

Chapter 2

FIGURES

The human figure and the diversity of form in nature and wildlife have inspired artists from the beginning of time. Painters, sculptors and other craftsmen have employed a variety of materials to portray the beauty of life in its various shapes, and forms. The earliest recorded figurative work produced by Royal Doulton was during the lifetime of the Company's founder, John Doulton. A flask depicting Queen Caroline was produced in about 1820, and in 1832 flasks were designed to celebrate the passing of the first Reform Act. The flasks and bottles were decorated with the heads and shoulders of those associated with the Bill – William IV and the Lords Grey, Brougham and Russell.

The craftsmen and women at Royal Doulton carry on this tradition, creating figures and animals from clay. The styles that our modellers and painters employ range from the realistic to the stylised, and in decoration the finishes span from plain ivory to the richly coloured, gilded and embossed. Royal Doulton is famous for the quality and fineness of its figures. The ranges are constantly updated. Figures are withdrawn and new ones take their place, each with her own special look and detail.

Figure and animal modelling is a constantly changing and evolving area. As you will see in this chapter it is also a complex and highly skilled business. Our professional sculptors Peter Gee, Robert Tabbenor and Alan Maslankowski are based at the Burslem studios and Graham Tongue with his young team of Warren Platt, Martyn Alcock and Amanda Hughes-Lubeck at the Longton studio, carry on an art that has been with the Company for over 150 years.

Ideas for new subjects come from a variety of sources such as our marketing department, our retailers, the public, club members and the sculptors themselves. There are topical events and historical celebrations to commemorate. Occasions associated with our Royal Family, such as the wedding of the Prince and Princess of Wales in 1981, are often marked with limited editions of figures. For the Royal Wedding we produced two pairs of figures, in editions of 1500 each, representing Their Royal Highnesses. In one pair the Princess of Wales (HN2887) is portrayed in her wedding gown complete with heirloom tiara, cascading veil and a copy of her original bouquet consisting of tiny hand-made yellow rosebuds (no more than 3 or 4mm wide), miniature stephanotis and other blooms. The Prince of Wales (HN2884) looks resplendent in the uniform of the Welsh Guards and is shown holding a sheathed sword, while beside him on a pillar lie his bearskin busby and white gloves.

In 1991, the 500th anniversary of the birth of King Henry VIII gave us the opportunity to create a truly magnificent figure portrait of him. In 1992 we commemorated the 500th anniversary of the year in which Christopher Columbus set sail from Spain to discover the New World. The Columbus figures are individually hand-decorated and numbered and include the signature of the modeller, Alan Maslankowski, on the base. They are presented in a luxurious blue, silk-lined case.

Spirit Flask, inscribed 'The True Spirit of Reform', made from salt-glazed stoneware, 1832.

My First Pet (HN3122, Alan Maslankowski, introduced in 1991);
Flower of Love (HN2460, John Bromley, introduced in 1991).

Ashley (HN3420, Nada Pedley, introduced in 1992); Kimberley
(HN3379, Tim Potts, introduced in 1992); Yours Forever
(HN3354, Pauline Parsons, introduced in 1992); Joanne
(HN3422, Nada Pedley, introduced in 1993).

Images figures. From left to right: Mother and Daughter
(HN2841, Eric Griffiths, introduced in 1981); Tenderness
(HN2713, Eric Griffiths, introduced in 1982); Peace (HN2470,
Peggy Davies, introduced in 1981). These figures were also
produced in black basalt.

Two Character figures by Bill Harper, both introduced in 1992.
Lifeguard (HN2781) and Guardsman (HN2784).

The Ace (HN3398, Robert Tabbenor, introduced in 1991).

I have personally collected the six models that made up the Gentle Arts series. These figures, limited to an edition of 750 each, were modelled by Peggy Davies, Pauline Parsons and Donald Brindley and were introduced between 1984 and 1989. The figures portray the pursuits of ladies of leisure in the eighteenth century. The topics covered are Spinning (HN2390), Painting (HN3012), Adornment (HN3015), Writing (HN3049), Flower Arranging (HN3040) and Tapestry Weaving (HN3048). The detailed work is beautiful and each has her own special metal accessory. The letter writer has a small desk on which her ink pot and letter lie, in her hand is a quill pen and on her lap a small spaniel. The artist has an easel with tiny picture, tubes of paint and water pots and the figure holds a palette and paint brush. The flower arranger is putting the finishing touches to a vase on a stand.

Recently we have developed a collection reflecting current pastimes. The characters include a golfing duo, Teeing Off (HN3276) and Winning Putt (HN3279) and Gardening Time (HN3401) all of which have become

Four figures from The Gentle Arts, a limited edition series produced between 1984 and 1989. Flower Arranging (HN3040, Donald Brindley); Writing (HN3049, Pauline Parsons); Adornment (HN3015, Pauline Parsons); Painting (HN3012, Pauline Parsons).

Detail of Writing (HN3049).

popular contemporary gifts. Another well received new line is Sentiments, slightly smaller figures in plain white dresses, with simple embossed decoration, expressing the messages Loving You (HN3389), Thank You (HN3390), Forget Me Not (HN3388), Thinking of You (HN3124), Sweet Dreams (HN3394) and With Love (HN3393), perfect to give or receive for any occasion.

We aimed to provide more than a gift with the pure white Images range. The idea was to create a gift that would also become a symbol or keepsake. Pauline Parsons modelled Congratulations (HN3351), an 11-inch high sculpture of a man and woman facing each other, suitable for many occasions such as an engagement or wedding anniversary. The smaller Bride and Groom (HN3281), modelled by Robert Tabbenor, is to mark a wedding and we have had

many reports of the china figures actually being placed on top of a wedding or anniversary cake as a decoration and later as a memento for display in the happy couple's home. Another in the series is First Steps (HN3282) showing a mother holding the arms of her child as it attempts to walk.

As well as the ranges available through our many retailers, the Royal Doulton modellers are also responsible for creating special lines. Collectors Club editions such as L'Ambitieuse, the figure of an elegantly attired socialite arriving at a ball and inspired by a painting from the French artist Tissot, are not available to the general public.

Limited editions can take a number of forms such as a strictly limited number or by a limited period of production such as the Figure of the Year. Once the edition is complete all production moulds are destroyed after use. Limited editions are popular with collectors and are often reserved or paid for before the piece reaches the packing department in our factory.

HOW IS A FIGURE MADE

I often see prospective purchasers pick up a delicate Royal Doulton Pretty Lady figure and study her, rosebud lips, gazing eyes and then the overall impression, but what they do not see is the team of craftspeople and the hours of work that have gone into creating that single model. I often wonder if they have any idea just how much skill is involved in making the figure that they hold in their hands. In fact some people think that I actually make the figures myself – if only I were that talented! I was in a store one day when a sweet old lady came up to one of the staff and said that although she liked that year's Michael Doulton figure she thought that the dress was too pale. She wondered if Mr Doulton would mind going into the back of the shop and painting her a figure with a darker skirt. In conversations with club members and customers I have often outlined the processes involved, but find that I cannot really do them justice without a sheaf of step-by-step photographs. I know

Three Character figures. Left to right: Old Balloon Seller (HN1315, Leslie Harradine, introduced in 1929); The Wizard (HN2877, Alan Maslankowski, introduced in 1979); Biddy Penny Farthing (HN1843, Leslie Harradine, introduced in 1938).

Christopher Columbus (HN3392, Alan Maslankowski). Introduced in a limited edition of 1,492 in 1992.

Lady Worsley (HN3318, Peter Gee, 1992), from the Reynolds Ladies series of four models, each in a limited edition of 5,000.

Detail of sleeve cuff and riding crop from the Lady Worsley model.

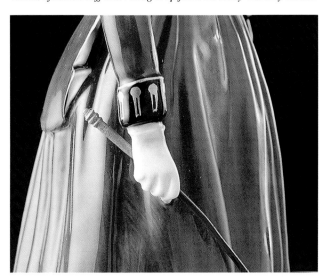

Romeo and Juliet (HN3113). The first in a series of Great Lovers, all modelled by Robert Jefferson and produced in a limited edition of 150. Others are Robin Hood and Maid Marion (HN3111), Antony and Cleopatra (HN3114) and Lancelot and Guinevere (HN3112).

Amanda Dickson, Director of Art and Design.

that those who have visited our factory in Stoke-on-Trent and seen the procedures for themselves are amazed. So I am delighted to be able to give you, with the help of these well illustrated pages, my personal guide to the making of a Royal Doulton figure.

The Studio Team

Our team of figure modellers work in a bright, daylit studio at the Nile Street factory in Burslem, Stoke-on-Trent. The young and lively Director of Art and Design, Amanda Dickson, has an office next door but spends a part of most days in the studio discussing new projects with the design manager and the the team.

Amanda has been Director of Art and Design at Royal Doulton since June 1991, and as such has responsibility for all aspects of design throughout the company. She oversees the design not only of sculptural items such as figures and character jugs, but also of areas as diverse as tableware patterns and cut crystal. Every new item bearing the backstamp of any of the Royal Doulton brands will have been seen by Amanda before it enters production.

Amanda acknowledges that the sheer breadth of the design department which she heads brings its own special challenges, working under considerable pressure directing the vast number of projects handled by the seven studios and more than sixty staff under her charge, with deadlines constantly in mind.

Amanda joined Royal Doulton in 1988 after studying at the Chelsea School of Art, having previously gained a degree in Art History at Cambridge University.

In the summer of 1989, Amanda was appointed Design Manager for Royal Doulton Sculpture, and at the end of that year became Deputy Art Director to Eric Griffiths. She acknowledges a great debt to a man whom she came to regard as a mentor, who taught her a great deal in the year during which they worked together. Upon Eric's retirement at the end of 1990, Amanda took his place as Art Director Sculpture, and six months later took over design responsibility for the whole of Royal Doulton.

Amanda is proud of the design team which she has established around her, for it is only their strength and enthusiasm which enables her to oversee such a diverse area.

A team of figure sculptors has been assembled in a new studio at the Nile Street factory, while the Beswick studio has flourished under the guidance of Graham Tongue. A new development is that each of the Beswick modellers spends time in the figure studio, working on figurative subjects and so broadening their modelling skills.

A recent and highly successful initiative has seen all Royal Doulton's studio sculptors spending one day each month at the Sir Henry Doulton School of Sculpture modelling from life. The aim is not only "to loosen them up," as Amanda puts it, but also to remind each sculptor that beneath the folds and drapes of costume, the essential form with which they are working is the human body.

Amanda believes that the responsibility of her Design Department is to be always putting something new on the table, to drive the Company's designs forward and to create successful design statements. Aware that new designs are aimed at the whole world, she travels as extensively as her schedule will allow, and spends a lot of time in Europe as well as visiting North America at least once a year. She sees a particular challenge in successfully blending the "Englishness" of Royal Doulton with the lifestyle, culture and taste of other countries.

The figure collection offers its own challenges, as the constant search for new looks continues. Ranges such as Images and Reflections have demonstrated Royal Doulton's commitment to expand the figure collection into new areas, seen most recently with the launch of Sentiments. One of the principal constraints placed on the design department is that every new piece must be capable of production in the Royal Doulton factories to the highest possible standard. One aspect of the development process is ongoing research into techniques of manufacture which have brought with them

Robert Tabbenor modelling Ulysses S. Grant from clay.

new design opportunities, and research is continuing into the possibilities offered by new ceramic bodies and other media.

The Royal Doulton modellers are exceptional in their versatility of style. As well as being able to model a range of subjects each modeller also has a speciality. Robert Tabbenor and Peter Gee have been with the Company for over eighteen years; both joined soon after leaving school and served five-year apprenticeships at the Royal Doulton studios. Alan Maslankowski has more recently joined the team on a permanent basis, having worked for the company as a freelance modeller for a number of years. Other designers who work on a freelance basis are Pauline Parsons, Valerie Annand and Nada Pedley.

Peter Gee joined Royal Doulton in 1973, aged 17. He trained under the watchful eye of Eric Griffiths. The first piece of Peter's work to go into production was the Catherine Howard Character Jug in 1978 and his first figure was Rachel (HN2936) in 1981. Many figures have been created by his capable hands since then. Most recently he has been responsible for two limited edition collections of ladies from the paintings of Joshua Reynolds and Thomas Gainsborough, each authentic in detail and scale.

When you realise that the figures are just 9¾ inches high (24.5cm) you may begin to appreciate the patience and skill of Peter's work in modelling the tiny pearl necklaces, lace-edged cuffs and gloves as well as the minute floral wreath in the Countess of Harrington's (HN3317) hand. The project required not only a great deal of research but also an ability to translate accurately a picture from painted canvas into a three-dimensional figure. 'I had to use a little artistic licence in designing the dress for Countess Spencer' (HN3320) Peter confessed 'because the original portrait shows only the upper half of her body. During my research I came across similar styles of dress and so I used a quilted underskirt, which was typical of the fashion at the time, to finish the figure.' Peter also found an unexpected partner for one of his Reynolds Ladies. 'I visited Harewood House in Yorkshire to study their portrait of Lady Worsley, but was surprised and thrilled to find another, uncatalogued, portrait by Reynolds of her sister, the Countess of Harrington. The Countess became the fourth lady in the series,' he recounts.

Robert Tabbenor has recently worked on the American military figures of Generals Grant and Lee for the Limited Edition Collection. His research for this project has made him a mine of information and incredible facts about the gentlemen. A clerk at the academy incorrectly recorded Hiram Ulysses Grant's name as Ulysses Simpson Grant. Hiram, rather than risk contention by correcting the error let it pass. His friends gave him the nickname Sam. American Civil War enthusiasts who worked in the factory supplied information about General Grant and the Civil War. In particular they supplied samples of grey wool fabric and buttons, identical to those the General would have worn, so the costume detail on the General's figure is as accurate as possible.

Alan Maslankowski, son of a naturalised Polish coal miner, is also a versatile modeller. He can adeptly turn his skills from large scale (both the 12-inch owl and cat in the Rouge Flambé range are Alan's work) to small (see the tiny bird in the hand of the Sentiments figure Thinking of You, (HN3124), see page 37) and from the historic Christopher Columbus (HN3392) to the more ethereal Pretty Ladies.

In the Beginning
When the ideas for new models have been discussed and

Ulysses S. Grant (HN3403) and Robert E. Lee (HN3404), both by Robert Tabbenor, 1992, in limited editions of 5,000.

finalised with Amanda Dickson, the marketing department and our Chairman Stuart Lyons, one of the modellers is assigned the task of producing a small figure otherwise known as a maquette. Few of the modellers at the Burslem studios use drawings as they tend to transfer the ideas straight from their mind's eye to the clay. Some background research and visits to the local library may be necessary if a uniform or a particular detail of a historical figure is to be shown. The costumes for Peter Gee's Reynolds and Gainsborough Ladies had to be accurately recreated, so drawings showing colour and pose were used for reference. Alan Maslankowski's 'rubble' base for the Limited Edition figure of Winston Churchill (HN3433) surveying the devastation of the Blitz also required drawings and the inspiration came from bits of bent pipe and discarded timber seen at a local rubbish dump. Otherwise the modellers are given a free hand to produce what they feel will fit the outline of the brief. Using the small, no larger than hand-size, maquette model for reference, further discussions take place with Amanda Dickson.

If the maquette trial model is selected, the modeller will then work up a full-scale figure known as a clay. It takes between ten and fifteen days to complete the master model but complicated figures can take even longer. Each sculpted fold and furl of material in a skirt or sleeve, each daintily curled tiny finger and neatly pointed toe is the result of many hours of painstaking work by the modeller.

The tools and equipment that the modellers use are quite a surprise. Alan describes his motley selection as 'bought, permanently borrowed and home-made'. He points out a few particularly strange looking specimens including a rather vicious-looking metal hook. 'Some are dentist's tools,' he admits, 'often the fine instruments used for applying fillings. Some I have created myself from bits of wood or smooth metal and others I have gathered from a variety of workshops and studios where I've worked in the past.'

The original clay model may be the only example of the subject ever created or it may subsequently be put into production, but whatever the outcome the detailing for each figure must be precise and accurate and, although to you or me the final stages of fine tuning may appear unnoticeable, they are of the utmost importance. A few years ago Peter Gee accompanied me on a tour of Canada. During one of his modelling demonstrations he started the prototype for the Confucius figure. 'In the first few days,' explains Peter, 'a figure really takes form quite quickly; it is during this time that the modeller knows instinctively whether the idea will work or not. During our Canadian tour the early venues saw quite rapid advancement in the forming of the grey, clay figure but as the days progressed, the changes in the model became almost imperceptible. During the last day I was adding the final touches, painstakingly smoothing each fold and crease in the grey clay garments with a wet paintbrush. One little boy who was watching me, declared to his mother in a voice so loud, that the whole store could hear, "Mummy, why is that man painting the figure grey?" '

When the clay figure has been finished this master model is photographed. The pictures are presented at another meeting with the Chairman, and the marketing and design departments, for final selection. Those that survive this meeting go on to the next stage – Mouldmaking.

Detail showing the head and shoulders of the Countess Mary Howe (HN3007, Peter Gee, 1992).

Countess Mary Howe (HN3007, from the Gainsborough Ladies series of four models, Peter Gee, limited edition of 5,000, 1990).

From Blocking to Production Mould

The clay model is then marked up by the blockmaker. A blockmaker works in the studio and can be consulted by the modeller as they work because there may be a pose, an outstretched hand or a curling skirt hem which will cause problems during manufacture. A blockmaker takes an indelible pencil and marks the clay figure into several sections indicating how many separate moulds will be necessary for production. The blockmaker then uses a sharp scalpel to cut into the clay model – a breathtaking moment for an onlooker, but a matter of course for these experienced and skilled craftsmen. One cut will remove the head and neckline from the figure, for example, a Pretty Lady, leaving the dress as though it were hanging empty on a coat hanger. Other cuts may be necessary to remove arms or legs that need to be cast in separate moulds. Finally the body and dress will be divided into at least two pieces. Most Pretty Lady figures are cut into several pieces.

Using these pieces a master or block mould will be formed from plaster. When the master moulds are dry they are taken to our prestige casting department. A caster will then test or 'prove' the master mould by casting and assembling the figure.

If the master mould passes all the rigorous tests, a blue rubber cast is made of it. This is known as a case. From this case hundreds of other production plaster moulds can be made. Plaster of Paris moulds last a limited time because water absorbed from the clay into the plaster and the regular wearing away by the application of the clay cause the detail and definition in the mould to become less clear. Therefore each plaster mould is replaced regularly.

Figures are produced using several plaster of Paris moulds. A figure such as Hannah requires six moulds, a total of nineteen parts. The production moulds have a limited life and new moulds are continually prepared from the rubber case.

Pouring slip (liquid clay) into a mould to cast the figure Hannah. After a period of drying, a skin of clay is formed inside the mould. Excess slip is poured away and after further time to dry, the moulds are opened up to reveal the hollow pieces inside.

From Mould to Masterpiece

The 'working' moulds are taken to the factory floor where a caster creates and joins the various pieces needed to form a figure. The plaster moulds are assembled and bound tightly together with either rubber bands or cord and wooden pegs.

Each figure is made by pouring liquid clay slip into an opening in the base of the mould. The clay recipe consists of the finest quality ingredients – china clay, Cornish stone and calcined bone ash. These basic materials are rigorously checked to ensure consistency and purity before they are blended in water to form a liquid slip. Bone china is used for the Pretty Lady figures because it gives a delicate translucent finish. If you hold an unpainted figure up to the light and look through the hole in the base you can see light

Hannah is carefully assembled by hand. The separate parts – head, torso, arms, back and foot are fixed to the main body of the figure using slip.

through the china. The slip is carefully measured into each mould. The porous mould absorbs the water from the slip until all the inner surfaces are lined with a coating of 'set clay'. The slip has to remain in the moulds for a precisely controlled time to ensure that the cast pieces attain the correct thickness and strength.

Excess slip is then poured away, the moulds are opened up and the various pieces are removed. The process of joining the pieces together is called sticking up, and if I were to work in the manufacturing side of the business, this is what I would want to do. I do not have the skill to be a modeller or the artistic ability to decorate but I enjoy watching the figures being put together. The experienced assemblers stick-up the figures using more liquid clay. With a Pretty Lady figure the head and neckline are fitted back into the empty dress, arms and feet are added to sleeves and hemlines, and soon a white clay figure emerges. I find it fascinating to watch them grow.

The assembled figure is then fettled or smoothed so that any joins or excess clay are removed. The figure then dries for a while to allow surplus water to evaporate. It has to dry slowly for up to four days because the figure is hollow and it would crack if it was immediately put in the kiln. Both the inside and the outside of the figures have to be equally dry before they can be fired. Many of the figures have to have specially made supports put round them to give additional strength during firing. The uplifted hems of skirts, raised hands, hat brims and larger figures, for example. Images are carefully supported by small columns of china clay. When school children visit this part of the factory they find it most amusing. I've heard them refer to it as the accident department because the supports make the figures look as though they are sporting slings and crutches. The supports can be used only once.

When dried and supported the figures go for their first or biscuit firing at a temperature of 1250°C. The figure reduces in size by approximately $12^1/_2$ per cent. The firing also fuses the assembled pieces together. When cool the supports are removed and whole figure is now in a biscuit state.

On leaving the kiln the biscuit china figure has a dull, matt surface. Depending on the type of decoration to be applied – under or on glaze – it is either passed directly to the painters for initial decoration, or, as for a Pretty Lady, is dipped by hand into a vat of liquid glaze. Glaze is a mixture of glass-forming materials suspended in water. After firing at around

First-Biscuit Fire. During the first firing at 1250°C all the parts of the figure fuse together and the clay changes from a fragile pliable substance to a solid biscuit-like state. The figure shrinks by 12½ per cent as water evaporates from the china clay.

1,050°C pieces emerge with a bright sparkling coating of glass which has become bonded to the china body.

Figure Decorating

When I visit the figure painting department at the Royal Doulton Nile Street factory I am always reminded of the little round sweets I used to love as a child. As you climb the stairs in the warm building, warmed by the heat of the kilns, the aromatic scent of aniseed rises on the air. Aniseed oil is used by the decorators to mix the colour pigments with which they paint the models. The rich scent, reminiscent of the aniseed ball sweets, fill the department. Although the decorators who work there every day hardly seem to notice the aroma, it always tempts me to visit a local sweet shop and buy half a pound of the hard, suckable sweets that leave red lines on the inside of your lips.

From the matt or shiny plain white stage, the figure passes into the talented hands of Royal Doulton's figure painters who will apply the fine features and high quality decoration that distinguishes Royal Doulton figures. The decoration and colours used on each figure are determined by the design department and any requirements for historical accuracy are carefully observed.

Figures are decorated by hand using a variety of methods. It is the end result which dictates the particular technique used by our skilled decorators. For instance, we can best apply an even rich base colour by fine spray rather than a paint brush. This technique is called aerographing. It always fascinates me how simple objects play an important part in the creation of our figures. Our hand painters place a wooden peg or stick into the hole in the base of the figure to keep it steady while the decoration is applied.

The paints used by the artists are specially prepared ceramic pigments and are mixed with not only the scented aniseed oil but also fat oil and sometimes a minute amount of turpentine or glycerine. It is Royal Doulton's subtle blending and application of these pigments that achieves the delicate harmony of colour for which the figures are renowned. As many of the colours react differently to firing temperatures, an intimate knowledge of the ceramic paints is required. Tones of colour have to be carefully built up, layer upon layer and some especially delicate effects require as many as six or seven firings. Dark colours are difficult to achieve. To get a good deep blue, a pale blue must be applied first, and fired, then the darker colour applied and fired again. Red is one of the most difficult and expensive shades to create. If a decorator was to paint the raw red pigment straight onto a figure and fire it, the result would be a dirty grey. To achieve a bright strong red, such as the colour used on the skirts of the Top o'the Hill figure, an application of 'Massey's Orange' is applied and fired. Then 'Harrison Pink' is painted on and the figure fired again. So next time you glance at a figure in a red dress, think of all the stages that were involved to get that colour right.

Faces of Royal Doulton figures are decorated by hand, work that is fine and detailed. Fashions for make-up can also be observed through Royal Doulton's figures. Before the First World War only ladies of 'dubious reputation' wore make-up, but in the 1920s brightly painted lips were all the rage. Royal Doulton's figures reflected these changes in style. Recent trends, since 1970, have favoured blue eyes more than brown and mouths are usually closed whereas in the past lips were often slightly parted.

Within the decorating department is a select team of ceramic artists who paint the Prestige and Limited Edition figures. Pieces such as the Reynolds Ladies and Sporting Heritage series are all completed by this experienced team. Some painters currently working at the Burslem factory have concentrated on this fine detailed work for more than 30 years. Vacancies in this department are rare and there is vigorous competition for the few coveted positions.

It is also in this department that the fabulous Princess Badoura figure (HN2081), which takes 160 hours to

Glaze is applied to the figure and it is fired again. Colours are then painted onto the white shiny surface of the figure (see top right figure). Hannah requires several shades of colour – including yellow and blue (top middle) and pink (foreground) – before the dress is finished.

The figures are placed in a kiln and fired to ensure that the colours mature and sink into the glaze. Often more than one enamel firing is required.

Fine brushes are used to paint the faces of Royal Doulton figures. After the face has been painted the figure will be fired again.

decorate, is completed. Made-to-order figures such as St George and the Dragon (HN2856), made in 39 individual pieces from 82 mould parts, and the Matador and Bull (HN2324), which are both from the Prestige range, are also painted here. The Matador and Bull was originally modelled in 1963 to commemorate the Centenary of Stoke City Football Club and a visit to the city by the famous Spanish Football Club, Real Madrid, who were presented with a model of the figure.

Other decorating techniques include the use of lithographs. These are sometimes used to give extra interest to a figure, for example, in the figure of The Wizard

Flowermaking: If flowers are to be added to a figure they are made by hand, petal by petal, and carefully placed in position.

(HN2877) the spell in the book he is reading has been printed onto a ceramic transfer, this is then applied by hand to each model of the Wizard during production.

Royal Doulton's research and design departments continually experiment with new decorative techniques. Once approved these will be introduced to the production process in order to maintain the high standard and quality of Royal Doulton figures.

The Finishing Touches

Some figures have special details that are added separately, but finished with the same painting and firing procedure as the rest of the figure. Many of these fine trimmings are flowers, held singly in a hand or in bunches, baskets and

Hannah (HN3369, Nada Pedley, introduced in 1991).

bouquets. Flowers have been popular on figures since they were first produced at the Burslem factory in 1913. Phoebe Stabler's Madonna of the Square (HN10) depicts a seated flower-seller nursing a baby, but the flowers in her basket are moulded and lack the individual petal detail that our current craftswomen produce.

At the Burslem factory today, a small number of highly skilled women are responsible for all the floral decoration. Finishing floral touches vary from a single bloom to full bouquets and demonstrations of flowermaking have been presented to The Queen, when she was Princess Elizabeth, and Princess Diana during Royal visits to the factory.

Detail showing the bouquet carried by the Princess of Wales (HN2887, Eric Griffiths, 1982). Fifty flowers and leaves were required to make up this bouquet.

Madonna of the Square (HN10, Pheobe Stabler, 1913-1938).

Flowermakers still use the same techniques introduced soon after the end of the Second World War. Every petal, stamen and leaf is individually made and assembled. The flowers are then arranged in a pattern designed by the modeller, but such a degree of hand crafting is employed that no two figures will ever have exactly the same flowers. The flowers and leaves are modelled from specially formulated clay that will withstand both delicate manipulation and high-temperature firing. To prevent the clay from sticking to her fingers the flowermaker keeps her hands moist with olive oil, a requirement that has the side effect of making their hands beautifully soft and supple.

Roses are the most popular flowers on Royal Doulton figures, but the flowermakers can produce many different varieties of bloom. The figure of Her Royal Highness The Princess of Wales (HN2887) in her wedding dress was undoubtedly one of the greatest challenges faced by the flowermakers. The bouquet held by The Princess was recreated using some fifty flowers and leaves, requiring over 100 individual pieces of hand-shaped clay for every one of the 1500 figures produced for the limited edition.

All the way through these processes checks take place to ensure that each part is finished to the highest standard. Finally each figure has to pass the rigorous scrutiny of the senior inspectors who will decide whether or not it will be seen by the collector or customer. The inspectors' keen eyes pick up tiny imperfections that you or I would not notice, but if there is a hairline crack, flaw, colour fault or a blemish in the glaze, it will be deemed unfit to carry the Royal Doulton stamp.

The figures are then individually boxed and packaged and sent to the shops and stores around the world who sell our Royal Doulton china. When a new line is launched I watch carefully in the shops and study the customers' reactions. The number of sales and the comments of both purchasers and stockists are then noted and I report back to headquarters in Stoke-on-Trent. These results are then discussed at our regular marketing meetings.

Names – Who Christens the Figures?

Some of the names given to the figures are inspired by a detail in the composition, for example Tender Moments (HN3303) is the title of a figure holding a tiny, delicate blossom in the palm of her hand. Loyal Friend (HN3358) and Sit (HN3123) are so called because the figures are accompanied by models of dogs. Ninette (HN2379) was inspired by the dancer Ninette de Valois and Isadora

(HN2938) by Isadora Duncan. The figures of La Sylphide (HN2138) , Giselle (HN2139) and Giselle, The Forest Glade (HN2140) were all taken from the ballets that inspired the models.

Research is also carried out to find the most popular Christian names of 21, 40 and 50 years ago. These names are given to figures so that the names may be appropriate to people celebrating a 21st birthday or 40th and 50th anniversaries, thus making them even more personal and appropriate gifts. Currently popular names include Sarah, Hannah, Ashley, Jessica, Amy and Emma. Members of the Collectors Club have also suggested names: Summer Rose (HN3309) is an example of such a recommendation.

The name of my Michael Doulton figure for 1991 may have been misleading. It was called Fragrance (HN3311), and in more than one country I have seen people picking up the figure to sniff it and being disappointed when there was no fragrant smell. But, who knows, that may be a development to look into for the future!

Withdrawal of Figures

Figures are sometimes withdrawn from manufacture because they are no longer popular or because the Company feels that an old style should be removed to make room for a new edition. The marketing department is faced with the unenviable and difficult task of deciding when a line should cease. The withdrawal of a figure occasionally causes the department to incur the displeasure of an unhappy collector who has finally got round to buying a particular figure, only to be told it is no longer being made. The general rule is that of supply and demand, and it is buyers who create the demand.

Fashions come and go, and colour themes that are popular for a few years are replaced by others, so that the demand for a figure with a green dress may have been high at the launch time but negligible a few years later. The marketing

A selection of figures specially produced for Michael Doulton events. Back row, left to right: Angela (HN3419, Nada Pedley, 1992); Fragrance (HN3311, Peggy Davies, 1991); Diana (HN3266, Peggy Davies, 1990). Middle Row, left to right: Pamela (HN3223, Peggy Davies, 1989); Laura (HN3136, Pauline Parsons, 1988). Front row, left to right: Kathleen (HN3100, Sharon Keenan, 1986); Nicola (HN2804, Peggy Davis, 1987); Wistful (HN2472, Peggy Davies, 1985).

department would note the decline in their sales figures and repeat orders from retailers and so feel justified in replacing that model with another, more topical design. Price can also be a deciding factor. Over the years collectors and customers have identified, by their buying behaviour, that there are price barriers which they are reluctant to cross.

A number of figures have been so popular that they are brought back in a different colourway or slightly different pose. One rather amusing example of a figure being 'adapted' to suit changing tastes or views of the times is that of The Bather (HN597). Modelled by Leslie Harradine, The Bather was introduced in 1925. She appeared as a nude, clad only in a shoulder-draped dressing gown. The model was inspired by the fashions of the period. By 1935 times had changed and in response to popular taste the later version of The Bather (HN1708) was produced with the addition of a painted bathing costume. The figure was exactly the same but the decorating department had a little more work to do.

There are occasionally lines that do not sell as well as we forecast. One example is that of the Tolkien Series. The small models of characters from *The Lord of the Rings* and *The Hobbit* by Tolkien were introduced in 1981 and 1982, but withdrawn in 1984. This short run was a disappointment to the Company but has made the figures rare and collectable amongst enthusiasts.

Michael Doulton's Figures

Since 1984 a special edition of a Pretty Lady has accompanied me on each of my visits. These figures are sold when I make a personal appearance in a store. Originally the figure was an existing model but with a difference. For example, the first figure was Gillian (HN3042), a figure already in production, but made distinctive for my edition by adding shoulder straps to her dress. Special colourways have also been created and more recently unique figures, not available in the normal range, have been modelled and introduced. I am frequently asked to autograph these limited

Left: The Bather (HN687). Right: (HN1708), Leslie Harradine. This figure was available from 1924 to 1949, but from 1938 most models were painted with a swimsuit in response to a change in contemporary taste.

edition figures, a task I gladly undertake, but one that has required me to develop a more legible version of my appalling handwriting! Signing pieces came about during one of my early visits to Richs department store in Atlanta, USA. I was talking to the floor manager as a lady shopper was selecting a Royal Doulton figure. The sales girl helping the shopper told her that I was a member of the Doulton family. The lady, who had bought an Old Balloon Seller (HN1315) figure, came up and asked me to sign it for her – it took about half an hour to find a pen that would write on the glazed base. Eventually a pen was found and that first signature started a trend. Since then, autographing has become a popular part of my shop visits.

A distinctive HN mark appears on the base of all Royal Doulton figures. These were the initials of Harry Nixon, a designer at Royal Doulton in 1913. The letters are followed by a number which denotes the particular colour combination used to decorate that figure. Other initials and words that appear on the base include those of the modeller and painter. The first figure decoration recorded by Harry Nixon was HN1, a figure of a small child in a nightshirt. The figure was also given the name Darling because on a visit to the factory, Queen Mary saw the figure and exclaimed 'Oh isn't he a Darling!'. The figure is therefore notable not only for the first recorded colourway, but also because its name was given by Royal Decree.

In 1985 the second Michael Doulton figure was called

The Royal Doulton backstamp.

Wistful. This was specially produced in a pale blue colourway and so was given the number HN2472 to distinguish it from the Wistful in the general range. The more widely available Wistful was in a subtly-shaded orange dress and had the number HN2396. Nicola was my lady of 1987, she had a pink and lilac dress with the number HN2804. The standard Nicola in a flame red dress has the number HN2839.

Other details about my figures may interest you. Kathleen (HN2472) available in 1986, was the first with a special Michael Doulton backstamp. In 1992 not only the colourway but also the figure was different as it was specially modelled by Nada Pedley. Angela (HN3419), holding the hem of her blue and pink skirts with a flower motif on the front, travelled with me from Inverness to Maidstone, from Cardiff to Bournemouth and from Canada to the Caribbean. The trend continues and 1993's figure was Sarah (HN3380), another specially modelled subject by, this time, Tim Potts, in a shaded orange and lemon gown with a vase of hand-made flowers

FIGURE MODELLERS PAST AND PRESENT.
It is difficult to find modellers with both the skill to produce the high standard of work we require and the flexibility needed to become a successful Royal Doulton modeller. When we recognise those abilities we do our utmost to encourage their work and advancement within the Company.

One of the earliest modellers in the Doulton company was George Tinworth. Tinworth showed artistic ability from an

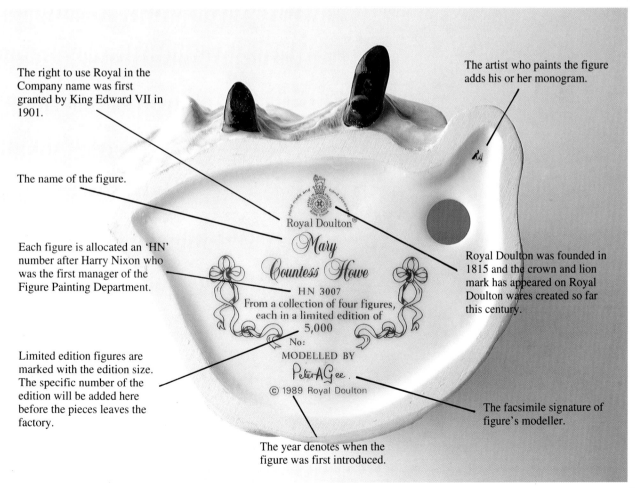

The right to use Royal in the Company name was first granted by King Edward VII in 1901.

The name of the figure.

Each figure is allocated an 'HN' number after Harry Nixon who was the first manager of the Figure Painting Department.

Limited edition figures are marked with the edition size. The specific number of the edition will be added here before the pieces leaves the factory.

The artist who paints the figure adds his or her monogram.

Royal Doulton®

Mary Countess Howe

HN 3007
From a collection of four figures, each in a limited edition of
5,000
No:
MODELLED BY
Peter A Gee.
© 1989 Royal Doulton

Royal Doulton was founded in 1815 and the crown and lion mark has appeared on Royal Doulton wares created so far this century.

The facsimile signature of figure's modeller.

The year denotes when the figure was first introduced.

early age, but was sent to work at his father's wheelwrights shop. It was not until he was nineteen years old that George found his way to Lambeth Art School. The principal of the school, John Sparkes, recognised Tinworth's talent and gave him a place. Tinworth gladly accepted but had to accommodate his artistic studies with work at his father's

The Jester (Charles Noke, 1893). This model produced in a parian body was in the group of figures launched at the Chicago Exhibition in America in 1893.

business. Henry Doulton, who had concentrated his early energies in the development of his father's industrial ceramic business, became interested and involved with the local Art School. Sparkes persuaded Henry to offer his prize pupil a job at the Lambeth Pottery, which Doulton duly did and in 1867 the Company exhibited at Paris a number of simply decorated saltglazed stoneware vases executed by students at Lambeth Art School on his behalf. The vases were well received at the exhibition. A similar response, four years later, at the International Exhibition at Kensington, convinced Henry Doulton that the Lambeth Pottery would be wise to develop this artistic side to its business.

Tinworth's early work was with large terracotta panels mainly on religious themes, many of which were used in cathedrals, churches and chapels around the world. From the mid-1870s Tinworth diversified from the large works to develop a new line of small modelled figures. These small figures were mainly of children, mice, frogs and other countryside creatures, portrayed in parodies of adult human situations and activities and are very popular with collectors today.

The man responsible for Royal Doulton's current figure production was Charles J. Noke, Art Director of the Burslem studios from 1913 but working for the Company from 1889. He re-established an early Staffordshire tradition and developed it into the ongoing success it is today. Noke also recruited one of the Company's most prolific modellers, Leslie Harradine. Many of Harradine's early models, some dating back to 1921, are still popular today. Such memorable figures as Sam Weller (HN531), Sairey Gamp (HN533) and Mr Micawber (HN532) are examples of Harradine's creative skill and artistry in making lifelike figures from handfuls of clay.

In 1912, after serving an apprenticeship at Royal Doulton's, Lambeth factory, Harradine had decided to emigrate to Canada where his brother had already settled and bought a farm, but during the First World War both brothers returned to England and joined a horse regiment. They fought in France where Leslie's horse was shot from under him, leaving the artist with a crippled leg. After the war Leslie Harradine settled back in England but, despite the pleas and enticements of Charles Noke, he would not come back to full-time work at Royal Doulton. Instead Harradine drew up an agreement with Noke confirming that he would produce figures for the Company from his own studio.

For the next forty years Harradine sent between one and four figures a month to Burslem. Some are still in production today. Top o'the Hill (HN1834), the windswept young lady holding on to her bonnet, was inspired by a Christmas card illustration published in the 1930s by Raphael Tuck. Another still popular group is The Flower Seller's Children (HN1342). These street sellers may have been inspired by the many flower vendors who used to gather around the steps at the base of the Eros statue in London's Piccadilly Circus. According to a story passed down by generations, Harradine is supposed to have come across the scene while walking in London late one night and is said to have sketched the scene there and then on the cuff of his evening shirt.

Within the last half century Royal Doulton have been proud to produce the work of a number of great modellers. Amongst them, and perhaps still one of the most collected designers was Margaret May Davies, better known to her hundreds of followers as Peggy Davies, who joined Royal Doulton's Burslem studios in 1939. Peggy had been a delicate child and bad health had prevented her from following a regular school career. During her bouts of illness she indulged her passion for drawing and painting. During one of her stays in hospital a nurse noticed the exquisite quality of her work. When other children of her age in the ward were drawing stick-people, Peggy was creating drawings that adults would have been proud to put their names to. The news of Peggy's talent spread through the hospital and finally her bed was surrounded by admiring doctors and nurses. Peggy also had a knowledge of clay and pottery from time spent convalescing at her grandparents' home in Longton. Here she saw men making saggars, protective clay casings into which pottery would be placed for firing in bottle kilns. The young Peggy enjoyed modelling with the scraps of rough, coarse clay the saggar-makers left behind.

After the Second World War Peggy became a recognised modeller in her own right and worked under contract to Royal Doulton until she retired in 1984. Amongst the best known of the many figures she made during her forty-year career at Royal Doulton are The Matador and Bull (HN2324), Indian Brave (HN2376), The Palio (HN2428), and the groups Dancers of the World, Lady Musicians and Period Figures in English History. Another of Peggy's popular groups, Les Femmes Fatales, included models of Cleopatra (HN2868), Helen of Troy (HN2387) and Lucrezia Borgia (HN2342) in limited editions of 750. The first nude figure for many years, Eve (HN2466), was also part of this collection. Peggy portrayed Eve offering Adam the forbidden fruit. The flaxen-haired figure stands in front of the fruit tree with the evil serpent entwined in the branches behind her. Her group of The Marriage of Art and Industry (HN2261) was the centrepiece of the Royal Doulton stand at the Brussels International Exhibition of 1958 at which Royal Doulton won the Grand Prix.

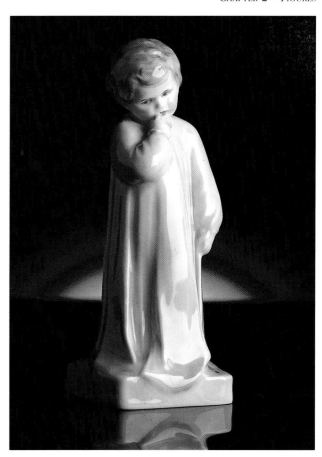

Darling (HN1, Charles Vyse, 1913-1928). A version is still in production today.

Another of our talented modellers whose work is still in production today was Mary Nicoll. Mary's artistic education was supervised by her father Gordon Nicoll, a well-known and gifted painter in oils and water colours. Mary studied at the Central School of Arts and Crafts in London and examples of her work were shown at the Festival of Britain in 1951. Mary lived with her husband and family in Devon and from her studio there she created characters and figures that mirrored the views and everyday life around her seaside home. Sea Harvest (HN2257), The Boatman (HN2447), Tall Story (HN2248) and The Lobster Man (HN2317) all convey the seafaring spirit.

Jo Ledger is not a name you will see on the base of figures as he was not a modeller, but he warrants inclusion here as it was under his leadership as Design Director that many figures were developed. Jo worked with Peggy Davies in the 1950s on Columbine (HN2185) and Harlequin (HN2186) and on the impressive figure, The Marriage of Art and Industry (HN2261). Jo was instrumental in the development of new shapes and decorations for Flambé Ware (see page 115) and responsible for new tableware designs.

Until December 1990, when he retired, Eric Griffiths was Art Director of Sculpture and many of his designs are still in production. He is probably best known amongst our American customers for his stunning collection of limited edition figures such as Soldiers of the Revolution and for his skilled portrait modelling which can be seen in many of the figures of the Royal Family.

Eric was also responsible for the introduction of the Images and Reflections ranges, which offer a contemporary

Flower Seller's Children (HN1342, Leslie Harradine, 1929-1993).

Figures illustrating contemporary fabric design, 1920-1965. Left to right: The Mirror (HN1852, Leslie Harradine); The Bather (HN1238, Leslie Harradine); Circe (HN1249, Leslie Harradine); Sweet Sixteen (HN2231, Peggy Davies).

interpretation of the more traditional figures. Amongst the many memories of his twenty years with Royal Doulton he particularly recalls drinking champagne and conversing with Laurence Olivier when making the model for the prestige figure of Lord Olivier as King Richard III (HN2881).

Bill Harper is probably best known for his Character figures and Prestige models including the magnificent St George and the Dragon (HN2856). The Clown (HN2890) and Punch and Judy Man (HN2765) were drawn from his own childhood memories. He is also a prodigious Character Jug modeller and has recently created a number of highly prestigious limited edition jugs including King Henry VIII and William Shakespeare.

Throughout its history, Royal Doulton has been exceptionally successful in finding and encouraging talented artists and modellers. From George Tinworth to our present team we have had some of the best in their field working for the Company.

Marriage of Art and Industry (HN2261, Peggy Davies, 1958), produced in a limited edition of 12.

Left: Two figures by Leslie Harradine. The Fat Boy produced in salt-glazed stoneware at the art studio in Lambeth, London, c1912; Carnival (HN1278, 1928-1938).

Above: George Tinworth modelled numerous studies of mice, frogs and other small animals in salt-glazed stoneware. The two figures depicted here date from c1884 to 1886 and are titled 'Hunting' and 'Play Goers'.

Below: Two figures modelled by Peggy Davies. Left, Fair Lady (HN2193, introduced in 1963). Right: Helen of Troy (HN2387, from the limited edition series 'Les Femmes Fatales', 1981).

Ninette (HN2379, Peggy Davies, introduced in 1971).

Top o'the Hill (HN1834, Leslie Harradine, introduced in 1937).

A selection of figures modelled by Mary Nicoll. Left to right: A Good Catch (HN2258, 1966-1986); The Lobster Man (HN2317, introduced in 1964); Sailor's Holiday (HN2442, 1972-1979); The Captain (HN2260, 1965-1982); Shore Leave (HN2254, 1965-1979).

Two figures from the Sentiments Collection, Alan Maslankowski, introduced in 1992. Left, Thinking of You (HN3124); right, Forget Me Not (HN3388).

Lord Olivier as Richard III (HN2881, Eric Griffiths, limited edition of 750, 1985)

Right: Sarah (HN3380, Tim Potts). The exclusive figure for Michael Doulton events in 1993.

A group of Royal Doulton animals in flambé and natural colourings. Courtesy of Phillips.

Chapter 2B
ANIMALS

Animals and birds appear in many forms throughout Royal Doulton's ranges. In my own home I have Strolling (HN3306), the elegant figure of a lady and her hound from the Reflections range. This figure was a present from my wife Pruna, because she says I stride too quickly when we're walking. The figure of Strolling is to remind me how the pace should be set!

My hobby is fly fishing and if Royal Doulton made china fishing flies, I'd collect them! I take a couple of portable graphite rods in my briefcase wherever I go and usually manage a few hours on a river or lake bank. I find that part of the joy of fishing is being in the countryside and bird watching is another pastime that prompted me to start collecting Royal Doulton birds. I have a number of Prestige birds, including an 11-inch high puffin which is one of my favourite pieces.

Pets are subject to the vagaries of fashion. During the 1920s the 'in' animals were Scottie dogs and our figure from that time called Scotties (HN1281) shows a Flapper girl with her two black Highland Terriers. A portrait of the Queen Mother as the Duchess of York (HN3230) incorporates her beloved corgi, a dog that gained popularity through its royal connections. The young Queen Victoria (HN3125) is also portrayed patting and holding her King Charles spaniels. An unlikely but voguish pet of the 1990s is the Vietnamese pot-bellied pig, a model of which has recently been created by Amanda Hughes-Lubeck.

By representing the special relationship between man and animals our modellers express a variety of feelings from friendship to caring. In our current collection Reward (HN3391), Sit (HN3123) and My First Pet (HN3122) reflect warm domestic scenes. The limited edition series Age of Innocence captures the nostalgia of country life and especially illustrates the appreciation of animals. The latest addition to the scenes, First Outing (HN3377) shows a young girl tenderly introducing her tiny kittens to the country world.

The most splendid, and most expensive animal made today is the magnificent elephant in gilded finery, on which the Princess Badoura rides (HN2081). The figure is 20 inches high (50.5cm) and was first cast in 1952 although the original was exhibited at the Wembley Exhibition in 1924. The Princess Badoura, inspired by the story from *The Arabian Nights*, is only available to order. The order takes months to fulfil because the figure has to be fired six times and the handpainting alone takes over 160 hours to complete (see illustration page 42).

Scotties (HN1281, Leslie Harradine, 1928-1938).

Animals are a perennially popular subject not only with artists but with collectors. They attract every age group from children who gather Bunnykins figures and tablewares to parents and grandparents who add to expanding displays of horses, dogs, cats or birds. My own mother bought for herself, the quite modern piece, Courtship (HN3525), featuring two white terns. She seems to have proved the point that there is no age limit to the appeal of these fine models.

Our models cover a spectrum of styles from naturalistic to stylised and whimsical. The Royal Doulton menagerie includes a great many species some wild, others tame and even mythical beasts put in an appearance. There have been hundreds of animal and bird models in bone china,

Queen Victoria (HN3125, Pauline Parsons, 1987). From the Queens of the Realm limited edition series of four subjects. This model shows the young Queen with her pet King Charles Spaniels.

Elephant and Young in a Rouge Flambé glaze (HN3548, Eric Griffiths, introduced in 1990).

earthenware and occasionally in Rouge Flambé and Titanian Ware (for further explanation of these glazes refer to Chapter 6, Artwares). I have a number of Rouge Flambé animals myself. I feel the rich glaze looks particularly good on the smooth, sometimes simplified shapes of animals such as the elephant, fox and especially the tiger whose striped coat looks so vivid in the black and red finish.

An interesting example of how a change in glaze and colour can affect the overall image of a piece can be seen with two models from the current Images of Nature collection. The first is Courtship (HN3525) which shows two white terns with their beaks almost touching, the other is Homecoming (HN3532), a model of two doves, one perched on a branch, the other with wings spread wide, just coming to roost on an upper branch. These two groups can also be seen in the Images of Fire collection, but instead of being glazed in plain white they have been bathed in the rich red and black Flambé glaze which gives a dramatic and showy effect. The Flambé version of Courtship (HN3535) sits beside my fireplace in our London home.

ANIMAL MODELLERS TODAY

Animals, bird studies and children's characters such as Bunnykins and Brambly Hedge are, in the main, produced by our young, specialist modelling team of Martyn Alcock, Warren Platt and Amanda Hughes-Lubeck, under the direction of Graham Tongue. Their small, friendly studios are at Beswick in Longton, one of the six towns which make up the city of Stoke-on-Trent. Visitors to the studios include dogs, cats and other small animals who 'sit' for their portraits to be modelled.

Graham Tongue originally thought that he would work as a coal miner like his father, but soon found his way back to the surface and trained as a tableware modeller. From the disciplined skill of designing and making tableware he graduated into the challenging field of animal and bird sculpture. Graham has been with the Royal Doulton Company since 1966 and like a previous Art Director, Charles Noke, he is a keen animal lover. He walks his Collie dog Jason each morning before work but leaves his other pet, Sadie the cockatoo, at home. 'I have loved animals and birds since I was a lad and I am very lucky my work combines my two loves, animals and modelling,' he says. 'Horses are my favourite animals and I have modelled a great number of them, including such famous racehorses as Red Rum, Desert Orchid and Mr Frisk'. This has involved not only meeting the horses, but their owners, jockeys and stable lads as well.

'The nature of animals cannot really be understood from drawings in a book or a single photograph,' reveals Graham. 'I always try to spend time sketching and photographing the animal from different angles and getting to know each one before I start to model it in clay. I once modelled a range of prize-winning bulls and, I must admit, I took very quick photographs of the top breed bulls I used as models because I wasn't too keen on being in the field with them for long. The study for the tiger model was one that perfected my use of telephoto lenses – I wasn't going to get too close to the real thing at Chester Zoo,' he says with a smile.

'It takes me about six weeks to make the clay model. When it is finished I take it to the stables or breeder for

approval. Often they can point out a certain look or position of the head that is typical of the animal and that slight alteration will make the model even more accurate. Sometimes the owner or stable lad will see a different dimension to their animal in the figure I have produced, because they are used to seeing their horse as a physical racing machine, whereas I look at it in a more detached way as a prime example of a beautiful animal. The finished model is then moulded and decorated. I also supervise the latter stage to make sure that the colour and markings are perfect. For some figures we choose a matt glaze which gives a non-shiny finish and looks more realistic, while for other figures we choose the shinier, gloss glaze.

'These days I make about a dozen figures a year, not as many as I used to, because my job is to supervise the team of modellers and oversee the production of our designs. The skills of commercial modellers are very different from those of a fine art sculptor. Our skill is to produce an attractive clay model that captures the movement and life-like details of the creature, but still make it to an appropriate size, acceptable for production and within a price range. We could make more complex models, but this would make the mouldmakers' task difficult and would increase the costs – so all these factors have to be taken into consideration.'

Amanda Hughes-Lubeck is a graduate of the Sir Henry Doulton School of Sculpture (see page 117), a charitable trust supported by the Company. The School encourages talented sculptors to develop their skills over a two-year

Images of Nature. Left to right: Gift of Life (HN3524, Russell Willis, introduced in 1982); Playful (HN3534, Adrian Hughes, 1987-1993); Going Home (HN3527, Adrian Hughes, introduced in 1982); Courtship (HN3525, Russell Willis, introduced in 1982).

course. Some of Amanda's recent work includes the Vietnamese pot-bellied pig, otters, badgers and a barn owl.

When I last visited the studio Amanda was sitting on a high stool by a small revolving turntable. On her turntable was the figure of a badger which she frequently turned and studied from every angle. She moved the head of the figure slightly from one side to the other until she found what she felt was the most appealing position. Amanda also sprayed the grey clay model with a fine jet of water, to keep it from drying out and becoming too brittle to work.

Beside Amanda sat Martyn Alcock who was working on a model of a fieldmouse clutching an ear of corn. Martyn, like Graham Tongue, studied tableware design and mouldmaking, but his first love is modelling animals. 'I learn something new with each piece I make,' said Martyn, 'Every model is a challenge.' Martyn gets a lot of feedback about his work from the factory floor because his wife decorates his as well as other models. 'She tells me which designs are difficult to paint and those which are more manageable,' he added with a grin.

Warren Platt is the senior of the group, having worked in the studio for more than six years. Warren came to Beswick straight from school and was trained by Graham while taking a part-time course at Stafford Art College. Now a talented horse modeller, Warren believes that one of the most important qualities of a commercial modeller is patience. 'You have to take your time when creating a clay model and, be strong enough to realise that, if a shape is not working it is sometimes best to throw the whole thing away and start again. It can be a difficult decision to make when you've spent three or four days working on the piece,' he said with feeling. 'In the clay modelling stage we have to exaggerate the muscle shape and hair or fur textures because these details become less distinct in the moulding stage. I

Figures from the Reflections collection, some models included animals. Left to right: Promenade (HN3072, Adrian Hughes, introduced in 1985), Cocktails (HN3070, Adrian Hughes, introduced in 1985), Fantasy (HN3296, Adrian Hughes, 1990-1992), Free as the Wind (HN3139, Pauline Parsons, introduced in 1989), Summer Rose (HN3085, Eric Griffiths, 1987-1992).

Princess Badoura (HN2081, H. Tittensor, Harry E. Stanton and F. Van Allen Phillips, introduced in 1952).

enjoy creating the anatomical details, especially the shape and action of muscles.'

Next to Warren was a sheet of paper pinned to a drawing board, and on the paper was a pencil sketch of an arc. Warren explained , 'I'm working on a model of a horse that will be one of a matching pair. To ensure that the two horses are the same size I have to calculate the amount of shrinkage that will take place when the water dries out of this clay model and when the copy clay figure is fired. The mathematical calculations will ensure that the new and existing models are the same size when they are finished.'

The modellers in this studio also have an interesting array of tools. Warren's bench-top collection includes a bent piece of aluminium and some fine hooks, the type used by hairdressers for separating hair that is going to be highlighted. 'Tools get better when they're older,' he says. 'The sharp or rough edges become smoother and they wear into the shape of your hands, making them easier to hold. Although I have over thirty tools in my collection I use only three or four on a daily basis, the others may be used just once or twice a year.'

The Beswick studio modellers usually sketch their subjects before working with clay. Photographs are used as an aid but the modellers feel that it is best to see the animal and note the subtle individualities that distinguish its character. For pedigree subjects the studio contacts recognised breeders. Once a policeman helped the team by

bringing his working Alsatian to the studio for a 'modelling' session. Many of the wild birds are modelled from live examples that are either hand-reared abandoned chicks or birds nursed back to health after an accident. These 'tame' wild birds are studied so that the most accurate representation can be made in the Royal Doulton model. A lot of attention is also paid to the bases on which the figures stand. A visitor to the studio may see a small pile of twigs, moss and stones on a desk top; these are carefully arranged to look natural and will be a reference for the modeller.

Work at the studio is varied; one week the team can be creating a new character for the children's ranges, Brambly Hedge or Bunnykins. The next week the brief might be for a racehorse or championship dog which can take from five to eight weeks to model. Although each modeller has a favourite subject, they all work on all the styles of models.

Right: Patience (HN3533, Peter Gee, introduced in 1987).

Siamese Cat, modelled by Mr Garbet, introduced in 1967, from the Fireside Model Series.

Open Ground, modelled by Graham Tongue. First issued as Pheasant in 1981 but a new base was designed and the subject re-launched in 1990.

A few animal and bird models have also been made at the Nile Street Studios. In the Images of Nature and Images of Fire collections Peter Gee modelled a heron entitled Patience (HN3533). All the models in the Images of Nature group are finished with a plain glaze or the Flambé finish which allows the eye to concentrate on the superb modelling of the forms.

MAKING MOULDS AND CASTING ANIMALS AND BIRDS

Horses are amongst the most complex items to cast. Legs, tails and ears are removed (as are legs and arms in the figures) (see page 25) and cast individually, then re-joined to the main body. There can be as many as 114 separate mould pieces for a Prestige or specially commissioned racehorse.

A blockmaker works in the studio with the animal and bird modellers. The blockmaker gives advice to preserve the best in the models, the movement and the spirit of the animal, but also to think about the other departments and their production difficulties. The blockmaker also decides which parts of the model should be removed and cast separately. There has to be an opening for the liquid clay to be poured into the mould at the casting stage. This space is usually created by removing a leg, but it must be easy to rejoin. There are on average thirty pieces of mould for a horse, each of which has to be carefully made and checked.

One of the blockmakers studies the model in preparation to creating the block mould. They look for 'undercuts', such as a curl or fold in a piece of material, which will require a separate mould to reproduce when the model has been marked into sections with an indelible pen. The technique is much the same as for figures (see page 26). By the time the first model is being cast in clay on the shop floor, the original model will be in the dustbin.

From the block mould a rubber case is produced and from this, in turn, are created plaster of Paris production moulds that will be used on the shop floor. Here the plaster moulds are assembled and lined-up on racks suspended over a trough. Into the mould liquid clay is poured and left to settle. When the caster judges that enough clay will have adhered to the walls of the mould, he pours out the excess into the trough. The excess clay is recycled and used again. A caster can make between four and five casts in a mould each day. But the number is dependent on the quality of the slip, the dampness of the mould and the size of the piece he is making.

When the mould is opened and the animal, for example, the horse Bois Russell, removed, the clay is still slightly rubbery, so it must be handled with care. At this stage a worker will 'peg in' or attach extra pieces that have been moulded separately such as the hind leg of a horse. The joins are 'made good', and smoothed so that they are indistinguishable from the cast body.

The clay pieces are stacked and left to dry, turning from grey to chalky white in the process. When dry they become brittle, 'Like a chocolate Easter egg,' one fettler told me. Fettling or tidying up seams and joins is done with a scalpel or knife blade. When the seams are removed, the fettlers give a final smoothing to the rims and edges with a wet sponge. From here the animals go to the kiln. They are fired at 1100°C

Warren Platt working on the original clay model of the small size Desert Orchid.

Horses are cast in several moulds – parts often include the main body, ears and back legs. These pieces are then assembled by hand, using slip.

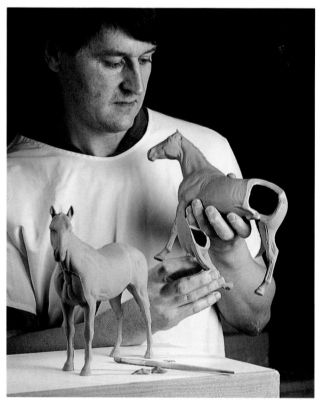

Two horses, modelled by Graham Tongue – Spirit of the Wind (introduced in 1980), and Springtime (introduced in 1983), taking pride of place in a teenager's bedroom.

for seven or eight hours. After the firing they are checked by a quality controller before passing to the decorating department.

Decorating animal models requires hundreds of shades of colour and a selection of these is used to decorate each animal. Every shade is subtly blended and applied to give the rise and fall of a muscle, the gloss of a coat and the spirit in an animal's eye. With a 'real' figure, such as the racehorse Red Rum, the colours and details have to be exact, as the horse is recognised by both his colouring and markings.

For animals matt glazes are often favoured over the shinier ones because the shine reflects light which distracts the eye from the subtleties of the modelling and colouring. The matt glaze is applied before the colours are painted on. One corner of the glaze shop is filled with rows and rows of shocking blue horses. The bright blue colouring is a harmless dye used to help us distinguish between the matt and shiny glazes. When the pieces are fired the colour will disappear completely leaving a non-porous surface for decorating.

Most glaze is hand applied by skilful technicians who know by eye and instinct exactly how much is necessary. Glaze can be applied by two methods, the first is by spraying with a hand-held gun and the second is by dipping into a vat of glaze which has the consistency of cream. Care has to be taken to ensure that the glaze is applied to every tiny feature and detail and in an even layer.

In days gone by the skills of the glazer and painter were taught by the 'Nelly' scheme. The foreman would tell the new recruit to 'Go and sit next to Nelly and see what she is

doing, then copy.' Nowadays the training is more formal and standards are higher.

As with figure modelling, Royal Doulton's animal and bird models were revived by the Art Director Charles Noke. It is thought that many of the early animals made at Burslem were designed by Noke himself, particularly the larger ones such as elephants, tigers, lions and leopards and probably the 'character' models such as monkeys, owls and foxes.

Amongst the vast 'aviary' of birds introduced by Noke can be found Baltimore orioles, bluebirds, blue tits, budgerigars, ducks, drakes, ducklings, owls, parrots and swallows. Other birds were modelled by different artists and include the exotic Indian Runner, British and North American breeds and domestic as well as wild varieties.

Noke was a dog-lover and so from the start dogs played an important part in the collection. The Championship Dogs series was introduced in the early 1930s but before and since there have been models of many other varieties such as Chows, Cocker Spaniels, Dachshunds, Pekinese and Fox Terriers. Our list is constantly expanding as breeders and pet owners approach the Company about having models made of their particular favourite breed and new breeds become popular.

Horses have also played their part in the repertoire since the 1940s when a limited number of models were sculpted by the well-known animal specialist W.M. Chance. His work included a model of 'Monaveen', a horse owned jointly by Her Majesty The Queen Mother and the then Princess Elizabeth. More recent additions include well known prize-winning racehorses and those based on the popular legends such as Dick Turpin.

Barn Owl (Amanda Hughes-Lubeck, introduced in 1990).

A group of bird models produced between 1900 and c1950.

A group of dog models introduced in 1990. Clockwise from left: Golden Labrador (Warren Platt); Golden Retriever (Amanda Hughes-Lubeck); Black Labrador (Warren Platt); Border Collie (Amanda Hughes-Lubeck).

Series Ware (see Chapter 5) also featured animals. Scottish Terriers appeared on a set of six plates. The Cotswold Shepherd with his lamp and crook is accompanied by his faithful Collie dog and a camel appeared in a supportive role in the Desert Scenes range. These are only three of the many different animal series.

Even cartoon characters have been transferred from sketches in magazines and newspapers to pottery figures. Popular examples were Pip, Squeak and Wilfred, a dog, penguin and rabbit from the *Daily Mirror* newspaper's strip cartoon. The mischievous Bonzo dog and cats Kateroo and Ooloo joined the other Doulton characters.

Mythical creatures also appear in Royal Doulton china. The limited edition Myths and Maiden series included Lady and the Unicorn (HN2825). A fierce dragon appears in the Rouge Flambé animals range, while another dragon is seen defeated in battle in the Prestige figure of St George and the Dragon (HN2856).

Other Prestige animals include Peggy Davies' magnificent Matador and Bull. Big cats such as Leopard on Rock and a tiger and lion also bear the Royal Doulton stamp, and so realistic is the lion with his flashing white claws and tense, sinuous body that you might expect it to leap off the shelf. I have models of both the Tiger and the Lion on Rock and find that each time I look at them I admire the quality of the modelling and painting.

Two special horse models. Left to right: Monaveen (W. M. Chance, 1949); Desert Orchid (Graham Tongue, limited edition, 7,500, 1992), available through Lawleys-by-Post.

HRH Princess Elizabeth (now The Queen) admiring horse models on a visit to Royal Doulton, Burslem in 1949, accompanied by Jack Noke, the then Art Director.

Advertising wares (see Chapter 3) have also been made in animal and bird shapes. A whisky decanter for the Matthew Gloag & Son Ltd, Perth, came in the shape of a grouse. Penguin Books commissioned a bookend of its mascot and the *Financial Times* newspaper commemorated Christmas 1988 with 'A Partridge in the FT' paperweight.

One of the most gifted animal painters in the history of Doulton was Hannah Barlow who worked at the Lambeth factory in London from 1871 until her retirement in 1913. Modeller George Tinworth who also worked at the Lambeth factory produced whimsical animal figures which are now rare and very collectable. A well-known piece of Tinworth's animal modelling is the Menagerie Clock. This piece is full of fun and mischief, and shows amongst other scenes the mouse band playing outside the wild beast show; the three card trick being performed in one corner; and a monkey hanging from a rope, while an elephant puts his head out of the side and steals apples from the stall of an outraged mouse vendor.

Hannah Barlow and her brother Arthur and sisters Florence and Lucy, were influential in the Lambeth studio. By their very presence at the pottery the Barlow sisters made a small but significant stand for the equality of the sexes, at a time when it was thought improper for 'nice' ladies to work. The Barlow sisters showed that painting was a respectable occupation and that it was acceptable for well-educated, middle-class ladies to have careers. Hannah Barlow's sketch books can still be seen in the archives at the Sir Henry Doulton Gallery in Burslem, Stoke-on-Trent. They are a fascinating insight into the life of this exceptional animal painter.

In contrast to her liberated approach to female employment Hannah still preserved the proprieties of a Victorian lady. Although she studied her own pets and animals at the public zoo, making copious sketches from life, she did not include their 'private parts'. Even udders on cows are rarely seen. At her own private farm Hannah nursed and tended up to a hundred small animals, from foxes and sheep to various cats and dogs. A selection of pets accompanied her to work at the pottery including a fox that was said to 'follow her around like a well-trained dog'.

Although the entire Barlow family decorated the Lambeth wares, Hannah and Florence were the most talented. By an agreement struck between the two sisters in 1877 Florence concentrated on bird painting leaving animal illustrations to Hannah. Their work is now very collectable. At my mother's house we have a number of Hannah Barlow vases and one in particular has been a long-time favourite of mine. The vase features a group of horses in a pastoral setting; the animals are so beautifully illustrated and given such life and character that it is easy to understand why she has become such a collected artist.

Vase produced in the art studios in Lambeth, London, from salt-glazed stoneware. Incised decoration of lions by Hannah Barlow, with additional decoration by Frank Butler, c1877.

Plate depicting a scene from the series 'Pip, Squeak and Wilfred', c1930. The characters were created by B. J. Lamb and were drawn by A. B. Payne and appeared in The Sunday Pictorial *and* The Daily Mirror.

Two jugs and a vase produced in the art studios, Lambeth, London, with decoration painted by Florence Barlow, c1880.

Vase, cattle in a pastoral setting, painted by Charles Beresford Hopkins, exhibited at St Louis, 1904.

A double-sided Character Jug depicting Sir Henry and Michael Doulton (William Harper, 1992).

Michael Doulton with Character Jugs depicting himself and his ancestors, Sir Henry and John.

Chapter 3
CHARACTER JUGS AND ADVERTISING WARES

I am a member of an elite group of people which includes Ronald Reagan, Sir Winston Churchill, Christopher Columbus and Mae West. I belong to the group because in 1988 I became the subject of a Royal Doulton Character Jug, as have all the others. It was a rather unnerving experience, seeing my features formed out of a lump of grey clay. The modeller, Bill Harper, studied me in detail – the cut of my hair, the set of my eyes and the shape of my mouth – then, without comment, reproduced each quirk and wrinkle onto the small-scale image. The finished jug gave me an idea of how other people view me. Looking at a model of myself was very different from seeing a flat photograph or reflection in a mirror. I do not often see myself in profile but with a three-dimensional jug I saw how my head looks from the side as well as behind! In 1992 a double-headed jug was launched with myself on one side and Sir Henry on the other, this has also been popular with collectors.

When I walk into shops and showrooms around the country I am often greeted by a shelf full of Character Jugs, and there I am staring back at myself. Customers have compared the likeness between me and the Character Jug and commented on whether or not they feel it is an accurate representation – I have felt in need of a facelift after some of the remarks I've heard. Other customers, who do not know who I am, have even told me that there is a Character Jug that looks like me. At our shop in the Disney World park at Epcot, I was amazed by a young child who said he thought the jug was of the former American vice-president Dan

Three Character Jugs. Left to right: Toby Philpotts (Charles Noke, 1937 to 1969); Robinson Crusoe (Max Henk, 1960 to 1983); Captain Ahab (Garry Sharpe, 1959 to 1985). Note the plain handle on Toby Philpotts and how the handle has developed on the other two jugs to tell part of the story.

A collection of 'firsts' among Character Jugs. Left to right: the first animal, March Hare (Bill Harper, 1989 to 1991); the first Character Jug, John Barleycorn (Charles Noke, 1934 to 1960); the first 'Royal', Catherine of Aragon (Alan Maslankowski, 1975 to 1990); the first double-sided jug, Mephistopheles (Charles Noke and Harry Fenton, 1937 to 1948).

Quayle. Another customer mistook my sculpted face for that of Prince Charles – I'm not sure that the Prince would be flattered! My step-daughters use their Michael Doulton jugs as pencil holders on their desks so I suppose you could say I'm always keeping an eye on them as they do their studying!

The Michael Doulton jug, with a handle featuring the Company's blue house flag on a flagpole, gave collectors an opportunity to add to the two existing Doulton family jugs. The others are John Doulton (made in 1980) with a handle depicting Big Ben opposite which the first Doulton pottery was sited. Early editions of this jug showed the hands on Big Ben at 8 o'clock, later models show the time as being 2 o'clock. The second jug is of Sir Henry Doulton (made in 1984) with a handle showing an 'Art' vase with coloured glazes and relief designs representing the decorative work pioneered under his directorship.

Character Jugs have held a special place in my memory because I can remember being taken to the Burslem factory by my father and painting my very own Character Jugs. As children we rarely made the trip from our family home in Sussex to Stoke-on-Trent because it was a long trek and involved an overnight stay at the George Hotel in Burslem – exciting stuff for small boys, but rather a strain for my father on a business trip. The Art Director at the time of our visit was Jack Noke (son of Charles Noke) and he arranged for us to have a tour of the factory and the showroom. I can

Henry VIII (limited edition of 1,991, Bill Harper, 1991). The two handles depicting the faces of Henry VIII's six wives are among the most complicated handles produced to date.

remember the thrill of having a go at painting my own Robinson Crusoe and Captain Ahab Character Jugs. I even had a special backstamp, including my name and the date, that was used to identify the two jugs. Alas I do not know where my Robinson Crusoe and Captain Ahab have gone.

Since Toby and Character Jugs were revived by Royal Doulton's Art Director Charles Noke in the 1930s there has been a variety of styles. These days there is great interest in the handles of the jugs as they are elaborately decorated and tell a story or add to the theme of the subject. For example, in the London Collection, the Yeoman of the Guard has a raven on a branch forming the handle. This pairing is significant because the Yeomen Warders guard the Tower of London and there is a legend that says if the ravens ever leave the Tower, a tragedy will befall the monarchy. Some jug bases have been extended to include not only the head and neck of the character but also the shoulders. The 1992 Character Jug of the Year of Winston Churchill includes the shoulders of his dark suit, white shirt collar and characteristic polka-dot bow tie. The handle on this jug depicts a Union Jack flag and a British bulldog, both symbols associated with Churchill.

Character Jugs can be found in four sizes, from the full size (7in, 18cm) and small (4in, 10.5cm) to the miniature (2³⁄₄in, 7cm) and tinies (1in, 3cm) versions. I have a collection of the tinies but wish I had been more diligent in collecting them earlier because they are now sought after and are getting more expensive to buy.

Another interesting variation on the usual Character Jug is the double-sided variety. The first double-headed jug was Mephistopheles, in production from 1932 to 1948. One side of the jug shows a smiling face, the other side shows him sulking. In 1983 another collection of two-sided jugs was introduced. The collection was called The Antagonists and had warring opponents on either side of the jug. The first were the Civil War rivals Ulysses S. Grant and Robert E. Lee, followed in 1984 by Chief Sitting Bull and General George Armstrong Custer. The next two introduced in 1985 and 1986 were Santa Anna and Davy Crockett and George Washington with George III. A follow-up to this range, The Star-Crossed Lovers, included the famous lovers Antony and Cleopatra and Napoleon and Josephine.

A double-sided Character Jug depicting George III and George Washington (Michael Abberley, 1986), produced in a limited edition of 9,500.

I have met Maureen Reagan, daughter of Ronald Reagan, several times. The first time was in a fashionable store in Beverly Hills. Suddenly I saw a tall, muscular man flashing his FBI pass at me. I thought I was going to be arrested but I was told that the President's daughter was about to arrive. Her bodyguards were very thorough and insisted on searching through my briefcase and checking all my pens, in

The Piper (Stanley Taylor, 1992), limited edition of 2,500.

Ronald Reagan, the former President of the United States, receiving the Character Jug depicting himself on 24th July, 1984 (courtesy, Bill Fitzpatrick, The White House).

case they were guns or bombs in disguise. Maureen Reagan has bought Character Jugs for both herself and her father and the family is obviously interested in them. It was with Maureen's co-operation that we produced a Character Jug of her father for the Republican National Committee. The modelling of the Ronald Reagan Character Jug was supervised by Maureen who came to our studios in Stoke-on-Trent. The jug was specially commissioned by the Republican National Committee to help raise funds for the James S. Brady Presidential Foundation. The foundation was established in honour of James Brady who was critically wounded during an assassination attempt on the then President Reagan. The Foundation provides assistance to people injured like Mr Brady.

Another special jug was modelled to raise funds for the Terry Fox Cancer Research fund. The young Canadian ran the Marathon of Hope with an artificial leg, having lost his through cancer. Terry's marathon run won the hearts of the nation, although sadly he died before completing the task. One of three copies of this Royal Doulton Character Jug was auctioned by Sothebys at the Collectors' Banquet at the Royal Doulton International Collectors' Weekend in Canada in 1990 and all proceeds were donated to Terry's appeal.

Another rare recent jug is one modelled on a schoolboy called Toby Gillette. Toby wrote to the popular BBC TV

Four Character Jugs with a marine theme. Left to right: Old Salt (Garry Sharpe, introduced in 1961), Neptune (Max Henk, 1961-1991), Lobster Man (David Biggs, 1968-1991), Captain Ahab (Garry Sharpe, 1959-1985).

Bill Harper with Mrs Fox discussing the model of the jug of her son, Terry.

Toby Gillette (Eric Griffiths, 1984), only three copies of this jug were produced.

Character Jugs from the Celebrity Collection. Left to right: W.C. Fields (David Biggs, 1983-1985), Louis Armstrong (David Biggs, 1984-1987), Mae West (Colin M. Davidson, 1983-1985), Groucho Marx (Stanley Taylor, 1984-1987).

programme, 'Jim'll Fix It', to ask if Jimmy Saville could fix it for him to have a Toby jug made in his likeness because of his name. Typically, Toby jugs are of old men, so we made three Character Jugs. One can be seen in the Sir Henry Doulton Gallery, the second was given to Toby and the third was auctioned for charity and raised over £15,000.

Characters from legend, history, fact and fiction are also featured in our regular ranges. In 1990 and 1991 a new small-size series of Character Jugs was introduced. These sports and hobby-inspired models are popular not only as presents to enthusiasts but also as awards to commemorate a sporting event. The six Characters are Gardener with his flowering pot plant handle; Golfer with flag, club and golf ball handle; Jockey with horse's head and finishing post; Snooker player with a cue, chalk and line of balls; Angler with a leaping fish and float; Bowls player with measuring tape and bowls, and finally The Master with a fine upswept moustache, in red hunting jacket and white cravat and horse head handle.

Looking through the shelves of discontinued Character Jugs at the Sir Henry Doulton Gallery in Stoke-on-Trent you notice a large number of characters from the works of Charles Dickens. The trend for these characters was started by Charles Noke. Charles Noke was a devotee of Dickens' work and so it was not surprising that characters from the pages of Dickens' novels found new life in ceramic form at Royal Doulton. Dickens' characters can be found as Series Ware and as figures as well as Character Jugs. Early models were by Noke himself, with assistance from the talented modeller, Harry Fenton. Among my favourite subjects are

Mr Micawber and Sam Weller.

In fact, Doulton's connections with the famous author date back even earlier to 1824 when the young Dickens, aged only 12, worked at Warren's Blacking Warehouse on the Strand in London. His job was sticking labels onto stoneware bottles of blacking. The bottles were supplied by Doulton & Watts of Lambeth.

In 1936 John Peel became the first real person to be depicted in a Character Jug and in 1940 Winston Churchill was the first contemporary person to be modelled. It is still rare to be modelled as a Character Jug while alive and the Beatles, Ronald Reagan, Toby Gillette and myself are amongst the privileged few.

As I mentioned in the previous chapter, Character Jugs are made at the Beswick factory under the watchful eye of Design Manager Graham Tongue. Graham has been responsible for creating a number of jugs, including Mr Quaker, for the Quaker Oats cereal company's 85th anniversary but most of the designs are modelled by two freelance sculptors, Stan Taylor and William (Bill) Harper. These modellers work from their own studios and send finished clay models to Amanda Dickson for approval. Modellers at our Nile Street studios have also contributed to this range. Peter Gee modelled Catherine Howard for the series of Henry VIII and his wives. Fellow modeller Alan Maslankowski provided the Catherine of Aragon jug for the same series. Robert Tabbenor created a regal portrait of Henry V for a jug launched in 1982, and also made the Buffalo Bill jug for the Wild West series.

During the 1990s a number of very special Character Jugs have been produced, and they clearly show the exceptional

Traditional British characters is a popular theme among Jug collectors. Two examples by Bill Harper are London Bobby and Lifeguard, both introduced in 1986.

Two small character jugs, The Jockey and The Snooker Player, both modelled by Stan Taylor and introduced in 1991.

The Canadians On Guard For Thee, a special colour edition of 250 commissioned by 'The British Toby' in Canada. Right to Left: The Soldier; Sailor; and Airman, all by Bill Harper, 1991.

Some of the many Dickens characters portrayed as Character and Toby Jugs between 1935 and 1986.

Character Jugs. Left to right: Juggler (Stanley Taylor, 1989 to 1991); Clown (Stanley Taylor, introduced in 1989); Santa Claus (Michael Abberley, introduced in 1984); and The Red Queen (Bill Harper, 1987 to 1991).

Two rare Character Jugs modelled by Harry Fenton. Left, The Red Haired Clown (1937 to 1942). Right, Pearly Boy (c1946).

detail and workmanship that Royal Doulton is known for. A double-handled jug of Henry VIII has the King as the central figure, but along the handles are the faces of his six wives, three on each side. Each tiny face is individually modelled and their head-dresses and features are delicately decorated. Another special jug is a three-handled model depicting King Charles I with a figure of his wife Queen Henrietta Maria on one handle and his rival Oliver Cromwell on the other. The third handle to the back of the jug is made from the feather of his Cavalier hat.

Keen collectors of Character Jugs trace missing jugs for their collections from around the world, and through auctions and specialists who deal in them. One of my most interesting and strange discoveries of a rare Character Jug was during a visit to Macy's store in San Francisco. I was seated at a very smart, leather-topped desk, in our department at the store, signing various Royal Doulton wares and chatting to customers when a gentleman came up to me with a rather scruffy-looking carrier bag. From the bag he produced what looked like a grubby plant pot in which was growing a large, prickly cactus. It took me a few moments to recognise that the plant pot was in fact a rare Character Jug of Winston Churchill dating from 1940. It is said that Churchill disliked this portrait of himself and told the Company to stop making it – so it was indeed a rare example. When I explained to the gentleman that he had a rather valuable and special Character Jug in his possession, his instant reaction was to tip the soil and cactus plant onto the top of the beautiful leather-topped desk where I was sitting. Then, without a word, he marched quickly out of the shop with his new-found treasure.

MAKING A CHARACTER JUG

The process of making a Character Jug is much the same as for figures and animals (see pages 25 and 44). When the prototype model is approved and finished off it is left to dry. The blockmaker then divides the model into sections and makes a block mould from the model. Most Character Jugs are made from earthenware clay which is a little heavier and more resilient than fine bone china. With Character Jugs the handles are usually cast separately. If there are any protruding extras on a jug, such as Winston Churchill's cigar, they will not work well in the mould of the body of the jug, so they too are cast individually. The jugs are fired at a temperature of 1200°c, cooler than for figures and during the firing they shrink by up to 12 per cent.

The skilful application of colour is undertaken by a team of painters. Many of the decorators have splendid arrays of brushes, probably numbering into the hundreds. When I asked one of the painters why she had so many brushes she replied. 'Because I've worked here for sixteen years and I have never thrown one away. You never know when it might just turn out to be the exact type of brush you need for a job.' The brushes are also expensive; some are made from sable hairs, others from squirrel and others from nylon. The stem of the brush is usually wooden but some are made from the quill part of bird feathers, now being increasingly replaced by clear, drinking straw-like plastic.

Each decorator takes a trolley of one particular Character Jug and handpaints a batch of up to sixty jugs. Each colour is applied to all the jugs which are then left to dry before the next colour is applied. The mottled, realistic flesh colouring of some of the more rugged characters is applied with a

Character Jug handles are cast in separate moulds and then fixed to the body of the jug. A skilled craftsman carefully reveals the mermaid handle which is to be attached to the Old Salt Jug. Note the Michael Doulton Character Jugs in the background.

Colours are painted onto the Old Salt model. The Jugs are then placed in a kiln to harden the colours onto the jug before glazing.

large brush onto the rough biscuit-fired china. The smoother, more creamy complexions found on the female characters such as the face of Henrietta Maria on the King Charles I Character Jug are applied on the glazed surface. Painting the eyes onto a jug is a very important part of the process because the eyes of the character create the expression and are, as the saying goes 'the mirrors of the soul'. What would take most of us hours to achieve is done with just a few deft strokes of a skilled decorator's brush.

Special paints and separate firings are needed to produce the metallic gold and silver details such as the silvery stars on The Wizard jug and cap badges and insignia on some of the military characters. Another technique known as 'scumbling' is used to highlight areas of decoration. For example, the 1993 Character Jug of the Year, Lord Nelson, has braid around the top of his hat and on the edges of his jacket. The rope texture was modelled in the original clay and is reproduced in the cast clay version. When the Character Jug reaches the decorator she applies a coat of brown colour over the braid on the hat and jacket. When she has finished applying the brown she wipes it off the surface, leaving the paint only in the 'valley' of the braid. When the brown paint is dry she paints over the whole area again, this time with a golden yellow, the combination of the brown shading and the yellow gives the impression of decorative, textured braid.

Old Salt is dipped by hand into liquid glaze. The glaze is coloured so that the craftsman can easily check that all surfaces are coated.

THE HISTORY OF TOBY AND ROYAL DOULTON CHARACTER JUGS.

'Toby' jugs were first made in the early eighteenth century. The body of the jug was modelled to represent a seated male figure with a broad smile on his face and an ale mug or pipe of tobacco in his hand. The rim or lip of the jug was formed by the figure's tricorn hat, each corner of the hat providing a pouring spout. The rest of Toby's clothing – his long frock coat, knee socks and buckled shoes – are typical of the time. No one is sure how the jugs became known as Tobys. There are two possible explanations. One theory is that the plump, rosy-cheeked figure of the original jugs was named after Sir Toby Belch, a character in Shakespeare's play *Twelfth Night*. The other idea is that a song called 'Brown Jug' was popular at the time and the main character in the song is called Toby Fillpot. The name 'Toby' became the general term used to describe this style of jug.

Toby jugs were produced by Doulton at the Lambeth factory during the nineteenth and early twentieth centuries and it was not until the end of the First World War that two Toby jugs were introduced at the Burslem factory. These, depicting Charlie Chaplin and George Robey, were made in small quantities and are now rare. Charles Noke brought the modelled jug back to popularity in the 1930s. His updated versions featured just the head of a character and were based on ideas taken from English songs, literature, legend and history. Noke designed his version of the Toby jug, called the Character Jug, to be stylish and colourful. The first to be introduced, in 1934, was John Barleycorn and since this date several hundreds of different characters have joined the range. In 1939, following on from the Character Jug success, a range of Toby jugs was launched.

In 1992 the first limited edition Toby jugs were produced. The edition numbered 2500 and the jug depicts another favourite Royal Doulton subject, the Jester. The Jester sits cross-legged and is dressed in traditional style with bells on the toes of his slippers, the points of his jacket and his two-coloured cap. A second limited edition Toby jug depicting the Town Crier was introduced in mid-1992, to be followed in 1993 by The Clown, in an edition of 3,000.

Toby Jugs differ from Character Jugs by portraying the whole body of the model instead of just the head and shoulders. Left to right: The Best Is Not Too Good (Harry Fenton, 1939 to 1960); Falstaff (Charles Noke, 1939 to 1991); Toby XX (Harry Fenton, 1939 to 1969).

Three limited edition Toby Jugs, all modelled by Stanley Taylor. Left to right: Jester (2,500), 1991; Town Crier (2,500), 1991; Clown (3,000), 1992.

Characters have also been depicted in other forms, and tea pots have been popular. The Old Balloon Lady was modelled by Bill Harper (1990-1991).

OTHER JUGS AND VARIATIONS

Many Character Jugs have been re-modelled or transferred to different body shapes to produce tablewares and decorative items. For example Dickens' Sam Weller has appeared in numerous forms – on jugs in a variety of sizes as well as bookends and as a musical jug, a sugar bowl and teapot. In the late 1950s tablelighters were a popular accessory and Royal Doulton produced them not only in the form of Sam Weller but also of Rip Van Winkle, Cap'n Cuttle, Beefeater, Falstaff, Long John Silver, Mr Pickwick, Lawyer, Bacchus and others.

The Toby jug style has also been used for advertising items. Charrington & Co, whose brewery produces the aptly named Toby Ale, commissioned Royal Doulton to make jugs in the early, seated Toby style. The head and shoulder style jugs have been popular with companies such as Pick-Kwik Wines and Spirits who commissioned a series of Character Jugs. One jug portrayed a character from Dickens' *Pickwick Papers* with the handle made to represent the Jim Beam whisky bottle. Another special commission was from Hampshire County Cricket Club. The Hampshire Cricketer jug was modelled by Graham Tongue to commemorate the centenary of their cricket grounds in 1985. These special and small issue commissions are sought after by collectors, because they are rare and in limited quantities and often not generally available.

Character Jugs have been a successful medium for advertising. Left to right: William Grant (Graham Tongue, 1986, for William Grant and Sons Ltd); Captain Cook and Uncle Sam, Graham Tongue, 1985 and 1984 respectively (for Pick-Kwik Wines and Spirits); Mr Quaker, Graham Tongue, 1985 (for Quaker Oats Ltd).

Bone china oval plaque depicting Queen Victoria and made for Vinolia Soap, 1897.

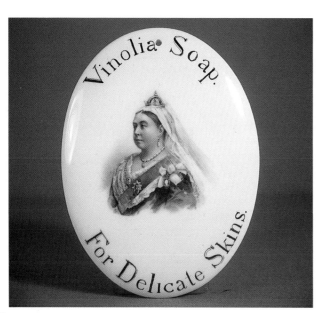

ADVERTISING WARES

This is a comparatively recent area for collecting, but it is fast gaining in popularity. Royal Doulton have produced many specially commissioned ranges for other companies and continue to do so. Early examples of Doulton Advertising Wares can be traced to the Lambeth Pottery where spirit barrels, ale, porter and ginger beer bottles were produced. The Burslem Potteries continued the business, and now these commercial, branded goods have started to reach considerable prices at auction. By their very nature, these wares are scarce. Many have been used in public places and have been broken or discarded.

Advertising styles are also susceptible to fashionable trends, so have to be updated and changed to suit the vogue of the time. As Charles Noke revived figure and animal modelling and the items became popular, so figures became prominent in the advertising side of the business as well. Products also change with the times. In the 1920s ashtrays had mottos that actually extolled the virtues of smoking. Craven A cigarettes boasted that their product was made 'Specially to prevent sore throats', and others urged 'Smoke, for your health's sake'. These days the demand for ashtrays

plaque from Royal Doulton, in the centre of which was a portrait of Queen Victoria – the sort of Royal endorsement that would never be allowed today. Even unattractive advertisments are collected. A series of plaques for Dr Scholl's Foot comfort services, featuring such products as bunion reducers and Zino Pads, are appealing to some.

Some collectors specialise in just whisky flasks or beer jugs. For them a source of inspiration can be found at a number of distilleries who have fine collections in their own museums. For example William Grant spirit flasks and bottles can be seen at the Glenfiddich Distillery in Banff, John Dewar & Co. Ltd have a collection at their headquarters in Inveralmond, Perth, while Whitbread's archives are at The Brewery, Chiswell Street, London EC1. In 1904 a Doulton whisky flask was produced in the form of a book to commemorate an account of the distillery family published by Thomas Dewar. This book was about his non-stop world tour which began in 1892. He travelled for two years and visited twenty-six countries promoting Dewars whisky and setting up world agencies. I feel as though I am following in Dewar's footsteps as I set off on my worldwide travels with my boxes of Royal Doulton figures – but travel these days is a much quicker and easier task than it was in Thomas Dewar's day.

The quality and charm of these old artefacts cannot be compared with some of the paper and plastic gimmicks produced today. Royal Doulton continue to exercise the same care, skill and imagination in the manufacture of their advertising goods as they do for the products in their own market.

Left, The Grouse, David Lyttleton, a flask produced for Matthew Gloag and Son Ltd, to the specification of Stanley Young, introduced in 1976. Right, Penguin Bookend, Martyn Alcock, produced for Penguin Books, 1987.

is minimal due to medical research finding that smoking is, in fact, bad for your health.

Royal Doulton Advertising wares could be found throughout the High Street in public houses, grocers, chemists and stationers. It is still possible to sit on a stool in some country public house and find yourself looking at an old Dewars stoneware flask or Toby Ale jug, or even putting a cocktail stick in a Royal Doulton Watney's ashtray. The chemist's shop was the place to find such items as a Wrights Coal Tar soap dish and shaving bowl. Yardley's Old English Lavender trademark depicting three flower pickers with baskets and aprons full of flowers was modelled as a 9-inch high pottery figure. Vinola soap commissioned an advertising

Figure commissions for advertising purposes. Left to right: HN582 advertising Grossmith's 'Tsang Ihang' perfume, 1924; The Sketch Girl, c1923, for the periodical 'The Sketch'; 'London Cry' advertising Yardley's Old English Lavender, c1925. All modelled by Leslie Harradine.

Biltmore, designed by Bobbie Clayton on the Georgian shape and introduced in 1991.

Chapter 4
TABLEWARE

Royal Doulton tableware is a daily part of my life. Each meal at home is served on Royal Doulton plates and dishes; even mid-morning coffee comes in Royal Doulton cups and saucers, part of a plain white service we use everyday. For more formal occasions we use either of our two services – Royal Gold or the now discontinued line, Gold Lace. My wife Pruna and I tend to favour the more classic designs, but there are many other dainty floral and abstract motifs from which customers may choose. I have also had a special series of fish plates made for my wife Pruna who is a keen fisherwoman. The set of six plates, each featuring a different native fish, have been painted for us by Albert Colclough, a Royal Doulton painter, now retired. Not only do they reflect our love of the sport of fishing but they make a unique addition to our dinner service.

My mother has whole, or parts of, at least seven different Royal Doulton services including a unique one with the Doulton family crest in the decoration. This special service was a wedding gift from the Company when she and my father married. On the occasion of my marriage to Pruna we were presented with a set of specially-made crystal wine glasses with double helix twists in the stems, created by another branch of the Company, Royal Doulton Crystal. The fine appearance of Royal Doulton's bone china is deceptive as it has great strength and can withstand the rigours of everyday family life, as my mother's collection clearly shows. Some of her services belonged to previous generations of the Doulton family and are still in use to this day.

Changing fashions and trends have influenced the development of our tableware. Shapes reflect the styles of the time – the 1930s favoured the angular lines of the Art Deco movement and in the 1960s the vogue was for rounded, informal shapes. Decorations also varied from stylised to traditional and pictorial. Typical of its time and reflecting the style influences of the era is Sweetheart Rose, an on-glaze tableware decoration manufactured in 1957. The ware was decorated with a lacy border and edged in gold. Sweetheart Rose was used by the Belgian royal family at the time.

Our glazes and china bodies have also had to keep abreast of the times. In the 1950s and 1960s new criteria arose. People wanted delicate china tableware but not as expensive as bone china. This demand for china styled for everyday use saw Royal Doulton's research team embark on a new project. In December 1959 the result of their project was

Royal Doulton tea wares from a catalogue dated c1905.

unveiled. English Translucent China, known these days as Fine China is as fine as bone china but considerably cheaper. In 1966 Royal Doulton received the Queen's Award for Industry for Technological Achievement in recognition of this development. Royal Doulton was the first china company to receive this award. This china has since become very popular although most people still regard bone china as 'the aristocrat of all chinas'.

Other changes in our homes and domestic arrangements have also had to be catered for. Today although some china

Bone china tea service with floral decoration in an Art Nouveau style, c1905.

Tea wares from the Art Deco period. Left: Eden (V1112), 1931-c1940, and right: Daffodil (V2050), 1939-c1945.

Tableware commissioned by The Ritz Hotel, London.

is still washed in hand-hot mildly soapy water, as it was in the past, most tableware is now subjected to the rigours of grease-cutting detergents, dishwashers, and the hot-to-cold temperature variation from fridge to oven. All these factors have to be incorporated into the china and glazes so that our customers receive resilient, hard-wearing products.

As well as the high-quality tableware available through shops and stores, Royal Doulton make special ranges for hotels and airlines, and individually commissioned sets. Our table settings are used in prestigious hotels around the world such as The Savoy and The Ritz in London and overseas hotels such as The Mandarin in Hong Kong and Raffles in Singapore. In smart hotels I have once or twice been 'caught in the act' of turning a plate upside down to check the maker of the china if I don't recognise it as being Royal Doulton's. In fact we have a Turn Over card club which we say gives the holder of the membership card the right to turn china over and read the backstamp. British Airways serve their business and first-class travellers on Royal Doulton tableware and a special bone china service and crystal glasses were produced for Concorde's inaugural flight in 1978. The first range featured a border design of small Concorde planes, but it proved so popular with souvenir hunters that it had to be replaced with a simpler, less distinguishable design. Individual china salt and pepper pots used on first and business class flights have also proved to be irresistible memorabilia. We have constant re-orders from the airlines for the thumb-size cellars.

Special commissions for costly services, some with rich raised and acid-etched gold decorations and fine hand-painting have been made. English and foreign royalty, Indian maharajas and American millionaires, as well as British and other Embassies have ordered their own special china from the Company.

Burgundy (TC1001, Jo Ledger, 1960-1981). Burgundy was the first in a series of six designs which launched Royal Doulton's revolutionary English translucent (now fine china) body. Others were Argenta, Citadel, Tumbling Leaves, Old Colony and Fairfax.

Tracery (1955-1964, designer not recorded), Bamboo (1954-1965, designer not recorded). These are typical of the stylised designs produced in the 1950s.

*Advertisement from 'The Pottery Gazette' of June 1881
describing the products of Pinder, Bourne and Co. It is
interesting to note that although the partnership with Henry
Doulton is not mentioned, his influence was undoubtedly behind
the doubling in production power.*

Although Royal Doulton continually update their tableware ranges, offering new styles and designs to complement the various trends in home interiors, established patterns such as Carlyle continue to appeal in all markets. Amongst our recent launches have been Claudia, decorated with a floral decorative border in a colourful blend of pastel pink, blue, green and apricot peony-style flowers and leaves. Biltmore was introduced in 1991. It features marbled sea shades highlighted with delicate diamond panels and motifs in gold. The pattern, designed by Bobbie Clayton, has rapidly established itself as an international favourite. A blue colourway, Stanwyck, has since been introduced.

In the fine china range, ideal for everyday use, we have revived an unusual octagonal shape and one of the most recent patterns in this shape is the attractive Marseilles design of fruit and flowers. An octagonal shape was also in production earlier this century and was decorated with patterns such as Old Leeds Spray and Norfolk, both of which are now popular with collectors of old tableware.

Our current expertise in tableware design and decoration is due to a continuing process of development that started in 1877. At that time Henry Doulton entered into a partnership with and subsequently bought the Pinder & Bourne Company. This marked the first stage of moving from London to Burslem in Stoke-on-Trent, as well as the start of the Company's involvement in tableware manufacture. Before the amalgamation with Pinder & Bourne, Royal Doulton had made drainpipes and saltglaze ware and latterly the spectacular Artwares (see Chapter 6). Pinder & Bourne's capacity as a medium-sized producer of earthenware tableware provided a new range of surfaces on which to apply the increasing number of finishes being developed within Royal Doulton's studios. Tableware was also a more

*Claudia, designed by Bobbie Clayton on the Palladio shape and
introduced in 1992*

practical and commercial prospect which would appeal to a wider market than the specialist Art vases and decorative items. Some of the Pinder & Bourne tea services, produced under their backstamp, were decorated with flowers and gold stippling, but Henry and his team soon replaced these uninspired ranges with new and exciting designs.

In 1883 the *Pottery Gazette* gave notice that 'Messrs Doulton of Nile Street Works, Burslem are commencing the Manufacture of china'. This heralded the Company's break from the heavier and more industrial business in earthenware and its advancement into the fine china ranges for which we are internationally renowned today. But the story behind the move into chinaware is not as simple as you might expect and it gives an insight into the character of Henry Doulton. Up to 1883 Doulton produced either stone or earthenware goods, but demand was increasing for the finer, more delicate bone china. This finer china was already available from Minton, Spode and Crown Derby as well as from many manufacturers in France.

John Slater and John Cuthbert Bailey, his two young managers, were keen to work with bone china but Henry Doulton was unsure. Eventually he agreed to buy some undecorated bone china from another Burslem pottery, Bodley & Son, but he stipulated that none of this china was to be stamped with the Doulton name. In the meantime a large order for tableware, to be painted by the Doulton artist Fred Hancock, was received from America. Influenced by a recent visit to France, Slater decided to order unpainted porcelain from Limoges. The china arrived and was painted but was accidentally given the Doulton backstamp. On an unannounced visit Henry came across these pieces as they were being packed for shipping. He flew into a rage and smashed the boxes with his umbrella. He marched into the

Eleanor, on cream body, designed by John Dennison on the Albion shape and introduced in 1993.

Lisa, designed by Hugh Saunders on the Albion shape and introduced in 1990.

offices where Bailey and Slater were working and instantly dismissed them. To add to his anger Henry missed his train back to London and was forced to spend an extra night at the North Stafford Hotel, which is still in business today. In the morning Henry returned to Burslem and greeted his staff with the instructions 'Send for the architect. I have decided to build a china-works'. You will be glad to know that

Juno, designed by Hugh Saunders on the Octagonal shape and introduced in 1988 .

Forsythe, designed by Hugh Saunders on the Classic shape and introduced in 1992 .

Regalia, designed by Hugh Saunders on the Palladio shape and introduced in 1988 .

Real Old Willow on the Majestic shape. This popular pattern is in rich Salopian blue and burnished gold and was designed in the late nineteenth century.

York, designed by Hugh Saunders on the Georgian shape and introduced in 1988.

Plate painted with 'Brook Trout' by J. Birbeck senior, 1907.

Five cups and saucers hand-painted in the Art Studios, Burslem between 1880 and 1900. Back row: cup and saucer from a design by George White c1886; cup and saucer, c1886, manufactured for Phillips, 175 Oxford Street, London. Front row: Cup and saucer, Pheasant painted by Samuel Wilson, c1893; Cup and saucer, Roses painted by David Dewsberry, c1910; Cup and saucer, Pomegranate design, c1895.

Bailey and Slater were reinstated and the incident was never referred to again.

At this time the area around Stoke-on-Trent became a Mecca for talented young artists. David Dewsberry, Percy Curnock, Edward Raby and Joseph Hancock were attracted by the growing trend for painted finishes on china and the exciting new opportunities in designing for factory-produced tableware. The artists were encouraged by a succession of Royal Doulton Art Directors, such as John Slater, Charles Noke and Jack Noke, to develop their own styles and specialist subjects. David Dewsberry is known for his magnificent paintings of views of Scotland as well as his detailed orchid studies. Edward Raby painted mainly birds and flowers and Joseph Hancock concentrated on fish, gamebirds and animals in their natural surroundings. Percy Curnock, influenced by Dewsberry and Raby, also studied flowers but is equally popular for his scenes from Italian landscapes. Many of these hand-painted plates were supplied to American customers. Percy began his apprenticeship under John Slater and Robert Allen in 1885 when Sir Henry Doulton was still a regular visitor to the studios. Sixty-nine years later Percy retired, having spent the whole of his working life painting his magnificent pictures on Royal Doulton china. One of his designs, Arcadia, introduced in 1946, is still available today.

The work of these artists can be found on many vases and decorative objects as well as on specially commissioned dinner services, fruit and fish plates. The paintings these artists created are so fine that when you look closely at the detail and quality of the work you realise they used the china base as another artist might use a canvas. I find such plates far too beautiful to eat from, they are objects of beauty to be appreciated rather than used.

Advertisement from 'The Pottery Gazette and Glass Trade
Review' *showing co-ordinating tableware and tea cloths, 1932.*

The basic vessel shapes and functions were also subject to change and experiment. Unusual developments included the self-pouring teapot patented by J.J. Royle, an engineer from Manchester. The teapot had an internal pump which meant that the lady of the house could leave the teapot on the tray or table and simply place the teacup under the spout. She would then pump the knob on the teapot lid and the tea would flow from the spout. The 'Patented Royle Teapot' was successful for a time and is said to have been used by Queen Victoria and Princess Alexandra. Another development was Gibbon's Party Plate which would appear to be the forerunner to our present-day TV snack plate. Gibbon's design comprised a tray, saucer and cup set which could be held in one hand. It seems that Gibbon designed the plate specifically to overcome a social dilemma which occurred at garden parties. The designer felt that his Party Plate would see that 'the least resourceful and most bashful of men cannot only attend to his own requirements but has an arm free to offer a lady'.

Between 1900 and 1930 some of the unusual glazes such as Lactolian and Flambé (see Artwares, Chapter 6) were used to decorate tableware. Titanian glaze with its soft pearly lustre provided a background on tea and coffee services which were further embellished by magnificent hand-painted patterns of exotic birds and fairytale or oriental themes.

Charles and Jack Noke both worked at Royal Doulton in the thirties. Jack, who finally took over from his father as Art Director in 1936, had a keen sense of contemporary style which he translated into tableware designs, for example the stunning Art Deco design, Deluxe. A number of Art Deco and modern style, earthenware and china tablewares were produced under the supervision of father and son.

By 1932 some of these china designs were sold with co-ordinating tablecloths, an unusual step at that time but one which has since become popular. Royal Doulton's advertisements announced the marriage of 'Miss Dainty Tablecloth' to her tableware partners of Dubarry, Syren, Arvon and Old Leeds Spray. The marriage of tableware to linens was innovative and a novelty which highlighted the fact that Royal Doulton intended their wares to be regarded in a fashionable context and as a way of integrating tableware with room decor. The Company wanted their china be sold at affordable prices, appealing to a younger and wider audience.

A large proportion of the Burslem factory's output during the thirties was tableware. There were mass-produced lines as well as the more prestigious gilded and specially commissioned services. Jack Noke's contemporary designs caused quite a stir and led to a number of special orders from prestigious hotels, such as Claridges, The Savoy and The Waldorf in London. These hotels commissioned their own special services with designs incorporating the first letters of their names. The Casino shape, introduced around 1932, was made in both china and earthenware. The simple, modern shape of Casino was remarkably advanced in combining both Art Deco ideas and streamlined form. Vegetable dishes were rounded, flattened and moulded to produce a gentle and elegant stepped effect – a very typical Art Deco style, similar to the steps of an Aztec temple. The manufacturing technique had come a long way from the days of hand-throwing.

Other designs for tableware, with names reminiscent of the era, included Tango decorated with a simple, understated

Brangwyn tableware c1929 to c1938.

rim banding and a semi-circular sunburst motif. This very refined Art Deco decoration was coloured in a choice of either gold, black and red or black, gold and green on white china. Also popular were Lynn, with a stylised Paisley design in black and green; and Glamis, Bella and Stella. The three latter ranges were decorated with floral and leaf motifs. Glamis Thistle to give the design its full title, was designed by Percy Curnock and based on a variety of Scottish thistle which grows in the vicinity of Glamis Castle, home of Queen Elizabeth The Queen Mother. One of the most unusual ranges to be developed was the triangular Fairy service. This china had a revolutionary, open triangular cup handle and simple cuboid bases to sugar bowl and milk jug. A popular decorative style, which is now a signature of the era, is the use of cool, silvery platinum banding. Royal Doulton designs such as Zodiac and Deluxe have this elegant finish.

Amongst the now keenly collected items of Royal Doulton tableware is a range called Brangwyn Ware. This was named after Frank Brangwyn, a well-known furniture, textile and ceramic designer who worked with Charles Noke on this special project for the Company. Brangwyn wanted to create a tableware that could be made and sold at a price that was 'within the reach of people of quite moderate means'; an objective he achieved, with tea sets for twelve retailing at £3 3s and a dinner set for twelve at £8 in 1930. The ware was made in strong earthenware shapes which were rounded, simple but with a heavy uneven appearance which deliberately imitated hand-thrown pottery. Decoration was in a mix of matt blue, pink, lemon, ivory, and a variety of shades of green and a golden brown colour. The outlines of patterns were formed in the mould stage, so colour could be applied over the outlines, creating an almost three-dimensional effect. Glazes were 'limp' and fluid to enhance the handcrafted appearance which also made it impossible to create identical finishes. No two pieces of Brangwyn ware were ever the same, not even 10-inch plates in the same dinner service matched exactly. The *Pottery Gazette* described the new line as 'another epoch in the development of industrial art'.

The *Pottery Gazette* may have been excited by the development but the customers that Royal Doulton and Brangwyn had targeted the tableware at, were less responsive. Brangwyn Ware was bought mostly by middle-class craft and pottery enthusiasts who valued it for its aesthetic qualities rather than the commercial price tag. The ware was not a commercial success but it is an interesting example, of what became known as, Manufactured Art Ware.

The orientally-inspired Flambé glaze was also applied to tableware but, as with the Brangwyn ware, no two pieces were ever the same. This did not prove popular with the general public who wanted each piece within a dinner or tea service, to match. Services in both decorative techniques are now fetching high prices amongst collectors because small numbers were produced and only a few have withstood the test of time.

As well as these innovative and fashionable designs the factory continued to make more traditional and floral styles. I have a coffee service based on a hunting theme from the Reynard the Fox series. The service is decorated with pictures of Reynard with handles made to look like hunting whips. This ware is now popular with collectors but my own collection has not expanded much of late. I wish I had concentrated on looking for the missing pieces of the set before it became so sought-after. Amongst the traditional and floral patterns of this period are the previously mentioned Norfolk, Old Leeds Spray (the original design is said to have come from the pattern book of the old Leeds factory) as well as, Countess, Watteau and Paget. These designs are now fashionable again and make a pretty addition to any country-style kitchen dresser or as a feature, grouped on a wall.

Today our designers led by Amanda Dickson, Director of Art and Design, also work on developing new sizes, shapes and colourways of tableware to suit the various requirements of our customers at home and abroad. For example we make several special designs for America and the Far East. For America we have designs which are produced on ivory, rather than white china, because that colour is favoured by our trans-Atlantic customers. The European market has a requirement for different sizes of cups. French and Italian customers prefer the smaller 5oz and 3oz coffee cups. The smaller coffee cups suit the Continental taste for drinking small, very strong cups of coffee, whereas the British prefer a large cup of weaker coffee with milk. The Italians also need large soup tureens, possibly to double as pasta dishes, so large, 6-pint tureens and lids have been added to the product range.

Collectors of current ranges include newly-married couples who may have been given part of or a complete Royal Doulton service as a wedding present. This initial gift usually leads to collecting more of the same service, whether to complete a number of table settings or to add a tea service. Many of the shops and stores that sell our tableware offer a Bride's List service. At such shops a couple can choose their preferred design and the shop will then inform wedding guests and well-wishers looking for a gift that a particular range is being collected.

The development of new tableware shapes and patterns inevitably leads to the discontinuation of older and less fashionable styles. In 1965 Royal Doulton stopped making earthenware tableware and this, along with the other discontinued lines, has become desirable to collectors. As a result of more recent tableware designs being discontinued a number of small businesses have been established to search out missing pieces of certain designs and services. These

THIS quaint decoration is reminiscent of Old Delft and represents scenes on the Norfolk Broads reproduced from fine engravings on an uncommon shape. The colour is a rich blue, which is enhanced in tone by the ivory earthenware; and the design being under the glaze guarantees the durability of both colour and decoration.

With its priceless traditions Royal Doulton inherits the skill and experience which makes it possible to offer such rare beauty at a comparatively modest price.

ROYAL DOULTON

FAMOUS FOR · SIX REIGNS.

Description from a catalogue of the Norfolk tableware design.

specialist companies will search out a replacement tureen, coffee pot or plate to complete a service or take the place of a broken or chipped item.

Opposite: Three blue and white tableware designs. From top: Norfolk (c1912 to c1950); Madras (c1890 to c1940); and Watteau (c1885 to c1950).

Royal Doulton

Octagon, D.N. 4209 "Norfolk."

Cecil, Flown Blue "Madras."

French, Flown Blue "Watteau."

SAVAGE, LITHO., BURSLEM.

HOW TABLEWARE IS MADE

You may think, looking at a large, flat dinner plate, that it must be a simple thing to produce. But behind the calm façade of our Burslem factory there are teams of skilled personnel following carefully-controlled procedures and processes that make each plate, bowl and saucer a special object in its own right. Like my ancestor, Sir Henry Doulton, I appreciate both hand artistry and the contribution of the engineer, scientist and technologist to create a perfect product which is affordable. We have a laboratory where raw materials are tested and a research and development department working with suppliers of materials and machinery to perfect systems. Indeed, our factories are recognised as leaders in the international ceramic world and I often wonder how the potters of old achieved their results without the aids available today.

In the same way that an original model is sculpted for figures from which the production moulds are eventually made, tableware items such as teapots and plates also require the creation of a prototype.

Tableware modelling is a distinct discipline which requires both an aesthetic sensibility and a precise and technical approach to work. Peter Allen heads a team of skilled craftsmen who are involved either in the origination of new shape design of the translation of those new designs into production pieces.

Whereas most figures are first modelled in clay, tableware uses plaster of Paris with clay being utilised sometimes for detailed work. In the development of a new range of shapes the first piece usually made is the coffee or tea pot as this gives the strongest style statement; other items such as the cup, cream jug and covered sugar bowl being styled accordingly. Simple machinery is employed to form the basic shape; a whirler (a sort of vertical lathe) is used in the creation of flat items such as a plate or saucer. Hollow items like teapots or cups are formed on a lathe in much the same way as a wood turner would fashion a bowl or chair leg. Spouts and handles and other ancilliary pieces are meticulously carved from plaster by hand. The blank-turned shapes are often only the beginning of a modelling process that might involve carving details into the surface (for example the flutes on an Arcadian teapot) or applying details to the surface in the form of finely modelled clay motifs or sprigs. Since the mid-1980s there has been a revival of embossed patterns on the surface of tableware so some of our recent ranges feature lines and shapes actually created in the clay, rather than being added only in the decoration after firing.

Size and capacity are a critical aspect of tableware modelling and have to be calculated prior to commencement of the modelling process itself. Allowances also have to be made for the amount that the china body will contract during firing and these calculations are included in the working drawings prepared by the tableware modeller.

After completion of the model the first mould or 'block' is made. Where possible a fired china sample will be produced from the block; this will be subject to rigorous scrutiny and may cause alterations to the original model to be made before approval is gained to proceed with the new shape.

A process now begins which replicates the original block so that the hundreds of moulds that will be needed for production can be made. Very simply, an impression of each of the original block parts is made from resin or silicon rubber. This impression is called a case and it is from this

A ten-inch plate being modelled on a lathe, known as a whirler, using a sharp metal tool to create the desired shape.

that the plaster of Paris working moulds will be made. Plaster of Paris is used for the standard moulds because it absorbs the water content of the clay. Plaster moulds lose their sharpness and definition after they have been used several times, so they are constantly replaced by copies taken from the rubber or resin case.

To make a plate from the plaster mould you need clay. Royal Doulton uses two basic types of clay. Bone china, the more expensive of the two has more translucence and is finer and stronger than the second type, Fine China. We also produce an ivory-coloured bone china, this is achieved by adding a special stain at the mixing stage so that the china body is cream throughout. The china clays are mixed according to specific and secret Royal Doulton formulas. The basic ingredients for bone china are: 25 percent china clay, 25 percent ground stone and an amount of fine calcined bone ash mixed with water. Fine China contains a proportion of fine sand instead of the calcined bone ash. The ingredients are mixed in a huge machine (a Blunger) until they are blended to the right consistency. The resulting slip is then fed into a press where the excess water is removed. Finally the clay press 'cakes' are fed into a Pug Mill where any air pockets are eliminated. If air remains in the clay, it will expand in the heat of the kiln and cause the plate or other piece of china to explode.

Tableware is made by two fundamentally different techniques. Flatware (plates, saucers, dishes, etc) and cups are formed on machines where clay is pressed onto the revolving surface of a plaster mould by a revolving metal profile tool. The face of a plate is formed by the plaster mould and the back by the profile tool. The mould is removed from the machine and placed in a drier where the clay piece starts to contract as water evaporates from it and is absorbed by the plaster of Paris mould. After about two hours in the drier the plate is taken from the mould. The dry plate is passed to the tower (pronounced toe-er) or fettler who places the piece on a turntable and deftly sponges the edge smooth and removes any marks or blemishes from the face that may have occurred during the making or drying. The plate is taken to the biscuit kiln where it receives its first firing at 1250°C. The biscuit-fired plate is checked by a quality supervisor and returned to another fettler for further smoothing and finishing.

Oval shapes, such as serving platters and dishes, are all hand-made because of the complexity of achieving a perfect shape. The skill in making these shapes is in spreading the clay evenly. The same thickness must be maintained all the way round the mould so that the platter is exactly the same thickness in the centre as it is at the rim. The dish-maker uses a special profile tool operated by a shoulder press, which, with the right amount of pressure, causes the detail of the mould to be printed onto the clay. Too much pressure and the clay becomes dented and useless.

The second method of making tableware is called casting and uses clay which has been mixed or blunged together with

---

Shapes such as teapots are cast using plaster of Paris moulds and slip. Sometimes the shape comprises several parts which are then assembled using slip. Here the spout is about to be placed onto the body of an Albion-shaped teapot.

water to form a liquid known as slip. This process is used for holloware such as coffee pots, cream jugs and vegetable dishes. The casting process is described earlier in relation to figures and sculpture, (see Chapter 2). Some shapes such as teapots or tureens may have parts which are cast separately, for example, the handle or spout of the teapot. After casting these will then be attached to the main body of the teapot using slip. The completed item is than towed or smoothed with water and a sponge and fired. When the biscuit-fired piece emerges from the kiln there is no trace of joins and you would never know that pieces had been added.

Most of the clay used in these processes can be recycled at any stage up to the first firing. If a plate is damaged, the raw materials are broken down and returned to the begining of the process.

There is an overall impression of whiteness in the flatware-making department. The casters who trundle the vast racks of plates from one end of the room to the other are dressed in white smock overalls and trousers. There is a rumble of conveyor belts and extractor fans and the intermittent clunking and rattling of the plates as they make their journey to the kiln or the decorators. Plate-making is done mostly by men because it is heavy work. Some of the larger plaster moulds when filled with clay can weigh over 55lbs and the pugs of clay are over 44lbs. The towing and finishing work is mostly done by women. Many of the people working in the business are related. You may find father and son plate-making, mother and daughter fettling or decorating and cousins, aunts and uncles elsewhere along the line.

In the past heat was a problem. When summer came a different work timetable was adopted, especially in the departments with kilns, where the heat became intense. The 'potters' holidays' (early and late summer) were a time when the whole factory, and many others in the area closed down. Daily working times were also adapted and a choice of working from 6am to 2pm was offered, so that work could be done in the cooler part of the day. Potters' holidays were always taken at the same time so that the whole business would close down. This was to allow the kilns to cool and repairs and maintenance to be carried out without large backlogs of china building up, waiting to be fired. These days we have many kilns and with modern technology they can be regularly monitored and maintained without disrupting the cycle of firings, but the tradition of potters' holidays still remains.

DECORATING

The first stage in the development of a tableware pattern takes place in the surface design department. The contrast between the shop floor with the bustle and clatter of machines, and this haven of peace and quiet, is noticeable. The main design studio is like a picture-book garden. The walls are covered with colourful posters, sheets of floral wrapping paper, postcards of famous artists' work, 'theme boards' of ideas, a veritable sea of colours and textures. Even the window-sills abound with pots of plants and flowers – all inspirational material for the artists who work there.

The sales and marketing departments constantly monitor the changing styles and demands for tableware through the remarks and sales figures of our retailers and customers' comments. The marketing department collates this information and forms an outline of colours, styles and price range that they feel will meet customers' needs. This outline

Dish-making using a plaster of Paris mould to form the inside of the dish and a profile tool to shape the outside. It requires skill and experience to produce oval dishes of an even thickness.

of ideas is given to the head of the tableware surface decoration department, Hugh Saunders. The brief is then discussed and developed by the senior design manager, John Dennison, and his team.

The other studio designers draw up their interpretations of the brief. Each designer has his or her own way of working. Some like to draw the designs in detail first and then colour the outlines in with watercolours. Others take straight to the brush and paint the designs freely without any pencil guidelines to follow. The patterns are created to scale inside a circular border that represents a large dinner plate. With fine pencils and pens they create an outline of flowers or more abstract styles or carefully-researched historic designs and with watercolour paints they create a full-colour version.

Then ceramic painters match the watercolour shades indicated by the designers, using the range of ceramic colours. It is a challenging task not only because of the subtleties in shading, but also because the colours change during firing in the heat of the kiln. Three or four plates are painted and fired, then the final selection is made by the head of department and marketing team.

Many interpretations are created from the original design brief. These variations are presented to the chairman, to Amanda Dickson and to the marketing department. The

design chosen will then be returned to the surface decoration department for further development.

The artists' skill is not only in being able to create a variety of ideas around one theme, but also in their aptitude for translating design ideas to a flat ceramic surface. Bobbie Clayton, one of the senior designers, created the popular Biltmore design which features a marble effect around the edge of the china. Bobbie's painted marble is, as it is in reality, different at every point. She created a design with soft flowing ripples of colour that vary from one centimetre to the next. It is such a cleverly executed design that it makes you take a second look to check that the plate has not actually been inlaid with marble.

Next door to the studio is the draughtsmen's room. In here skilled technicians work with the plate border design to make it fit onto the other shapes and sizes of china that will make up the range. Sometimes the draughtsmen have to scale down and cut the original designs. For example a floral border designed for a 10-inch plate will have to be 'pruned' to fit around the neck of a small milk jug. The skill of the job is to be able to remove parts of the design yet still make them look the same as the main dinner plate, which carries the whole design. The draughtsmen trim and cut the paper patterns with sharp scalpels. They take out tiny 'V' shaped nicks – like making wallpaper fit around a light switch – and ease the sides of the 'V' back together again. This process enables them to make a flat plate design work around the rim of a rounded and curved bowl. They then produce the final drawings which go to Royal Doulton's printing department for translation into ceramic transfers.

From over three months work on designs for the United Kingdom market, perhaps only two new designs will go into production. Only the very best bears the Royal Doulton name.

Hugh Saunders, who has been with the Company for over twenty-two years, also takes his work home. Hugh uses two Royal Doulton dinner services, but these, Carnation and Lincoln, are his own designs. Hugh has also created a very special range of tea cups and saucers for the Japanese market named after artists associated with Royal Doulton. The first is Curnock, named after Percy Curnock who painted decorative china for Royal Doulton in the early 1900s. Percy was presented to H.R.H. Princess Elizabeth (now The Queen) when she visited the factory in 1949, and was awarded the M.B.E. in 1954. The Curnock cup and saucer are decorated with finely painted flowers, including Percy's own favourite bloom the rose, with heartsease and other wild flowers. The china has burnished gold on the lip, foot and handle creating an overall impression of Victorian style.

The second in the collection is Sutton, named after Frederick Sutton, a talented artist who worked in the Royal Doulton Art Studios from 1898 until 1913. The Sutton cup and saucer are embellished with French neo-classical designs of bows and swags of roses. As with the Curnock design, the inspiration came from Sutton's own work using eighteenth-century miniatures and historical subjects.

The last of the group is Birbeck, designed by Donna Highfield. It is named in memory of Joseph Birbeck who worked for Royal Doulton from 1900 until 1926. The design for this set is in the Edwardian style and combines rich shades of blue and delicate gold tracery with stylised

A draughtsman at work cutting up a new design in order to make it fit every shape in the range.

Three designs specially produced for the Japanese market. From left to right: Curnock, Birbeck and Sutton. All three patterns were based on archive designs.

Once a design has been approved it is printed onto a ceramic transfer known as a lithograph. These are placed into position by hand by skilled craftswomen. Carlyle is the pattern being decorated in this picture.

acanthus leaves. Birbeck worked at Royal Doulton when Edward VII awarded the Company the Royal Warrant, an exciting and progressive time during which many dramatic and unusual designs were introduced.

When Hugh Saunders and the others involved have approved a new decoration the actual process of applying the decoration to the whole dinner and tea service passes to the shop floor. The decorating departments are filled with teams of ladies applying the various decorative finishes.

One technique is the application of lithograph designs. These come as transfers on sheets of paper. The china onto which the decoration will be put is kept warm in heated cupboards beside each lady and this aids the application of the lithograph. In front of her is a tray of soapy water, in which she submerges the sheet of lithograph. The soapy water makes it easy to remove the transfer and slide it into position on the plate. Guide lines are occasionally drawn on with ink and a compass by 'sketch liners' in another department. These help the decorator achieve the exact placing of the lithograph on the china. The pattern must be put a few millimetres from the edge of the plate to allow room for the gilded or coloured edge line. The fine ink lines

put on by the sketch liners burn away and become invisible during the kiln firing which takes place later. Transfers are pressed into place using a rubber disc known as a squeegy. Gentle pressure and the smoothing action squeezes the air out from under the transfer and ensures the complete design adheres to the china. The plate is then fired and the protective plastic backing of the transfer burns away and the colour fuses with the glaze.

The special gold and platinum finishes on our tableware are applied by skilled gilders. A team of ladies sit at individual benches with pen-fine paintbrushes resting in glass 'shells' which look like ashtrays with a stem. The glass shells are filled with unattractive brown and black liquids. The ladies busily apply fine black lines around the rims and handles of plates, cups and jugs. The finest lines are made using brushes that are so thin, they have no more than half a dozen hairs. The dull black and brown lines contain gold or platinum mixed with linseed oil. The oil makes the precious metals easier to apply. Silver is never used because it tarnishes too easily. The black oil burns off during firing in the kiln, leaving the gold or platinum firmly adhered to the china. The gold and platinum decoration is then sent to be checked by a quality controller before going to the kiln for a final firing at 800°C for four hours. The precious metal lines and decorations are a little dull after firing so they are burnished and polished with an abrasive pad until they become brilliant. Every item is checked again before being sent to the packing department.

Some of the finest and most expensive decoration on tableware is raised gold paste. This technique involves painting fine paste forming a raised design onto a plain plate. These designs of arabesques, flowers or fine dots are then gilded with real gold. As with the gold and platinum decoration described before, the precious metals are mixed with linseed oil for application. The decorated china is fired and the raised paste gold design becomes fused.

In the studios where this gold and platinum decoration is applied, the bottles of precious metals suspended in oil are kept constantly revolving on small rows of rollers. This ensures that the oil and gold or platinum are evenly mixed. At the end of the day the white cotton cloths that the gilders use to wipe their brushes and any drips or mistakes are taken away and carefully cleaned. All the traces of the costly gold are removed from the cloths and carefully put back into the bottles to be used again.

Another type of elaborate gold decoration is known as the Acid Gold Process and it is the style of decoration used on my own Royal Gold dinner service. The effect is traditional and stylish but still very popular. The process of etching delicate patterns into the bone china using acid and gold was patented by James Leigh-Hughes in 1863. Hughes was a gilder at the Minton factory and subsequently sold his invention for use at Minton. The technique gave Minton an early lead in the production of prestige tableware with a gold bas-relief finish but later Royal Doulton began to use the process and the Company made swift headway in the market. Many Royal Doulton designs using the acid-etched

gold decorating technique were produced between 1900 and 1930, but fewer are made today, due to cost and a decline in demand. Our own Royal Gold service, which graces the dining table at home on highdays and holidays, is an example of gilded ware at its best.

Acid etching creates a textured design within a gold band. The rich, delicate effect is obtained by using a black bitumin transfer. Bitumin is used because it is resistant to acid. When the bitumin transfer has been carefully positioned the whole plate is dipped into a bath of hydrofluoric acid. The acid 'eats' into the areas not covered by the transfer, leaving a design engraved into the china. The acid is rinsed off and the etched design is highlighted with 22-carat gold. The gold is fired to make it permanent, then polished and burnished with a bloodstone, a semi-precious stone which gives the best finish for this particular technique. As with all other wares produced by Royal Doulton, each item of tableware passes through a quality control check at all stages.

Amongst recent developments is Lambethware, launched in 1974. This is an oven-to-table range, designed to suit contemporary living. It is machine washable, oven, freezer and detergent proof yet still delicate enough to grace a dining table. As the name implies Lambethware was inspired by the Doulton Lambeth stoneware tradition.

In 1984, we sent the first bone china into space. Three

The final stage in the production process is to gild the pieces. This is done by hand, using a fine brush, to add gold or platinum lines to the edges and handles.

bone china plates went around the world 92 times on the space shuttle *Discovery*. The shuttle was named after Captain Scott's ship *Discovery* which sailed to the Antarctic in 1901. Royal Doulton supplied the tableware for the ship decorated with a penguin. It was thus appropriate that Royal Doulton should also supply china for the first expedition of the shuttle *Discovery*. A penguin was incorporated into the logo of the design on the three plates sent into space and also on pieces made to commemorate the event.

Following his return to earth Commander Henry Hartsfield presented one of the three plates to the Sir Henry Doulton Gallery. The second went to Captain Scott's ship in Dundee and the third was retained by NASA.

More recently Expressions tableware has been launched. This tableware is practical and can be used in the microwave, dishwasher, oven and freezer. Designs available include Amethyst, Summer Carnival, Florentina, Windermere and Strawberry Fayre!

In 1988 an octagonal-shaped oven-to-tableware was introduced. Extensive tests and research by the Company's development team resulted in a product which can be used in a microwave or conventional oven, in a dishwasher and freezer, and which is chip-resistant. The designs are suitable for casual or formal dining – the range is as useful in the kitchen as in the dining room and offers a new concept for Royal Doulton tableware for everyday use.

The initial collection was comprised of thirty-five shapes

A decoration of stylised flowers in dark blue and deep pink 'Windermere' from the 'Expressions' range of fine china is completed with a blue edge line.

in five different patterns or in plain white. This has now increased to thirty-eight shapes and twelve patterns. Some shapes, such as the quiche dish and pie plate, have not previously been used by the Company. Every piece within the range picks up the octagonal shape in some form – even to the knobs on coffee and teapots.

A commemorative reproduction of the design which was carried
on Captain Scott's ship Discovery *in 1901, 1984.*

The Discovery plate which travelled around the World 92 times
on the space shuttle Discovery, *1984.*

A plate from the Gnomes series, Charles Noke, 1927-1950.

Chapter 5
SERIES WARE AND NURSERYWARE

The concept of Series Ware was once again the brainchild of Royal Doulton's Art Director Charles Noke and can be traced back to 1899. The idea was to produce a range of china linked by a pictorial theme. The ware was originally referred to as Fancy Lines and was designed to 'solve the problem of the inexpensive small gift'. Series Ware would 'adorn, yet serve some useful purpose,' according to an advertisement from the turn of the century. Noke in fact launched the ultimate collectable range. You could give one piece and add to it at the next occasion, eventually building up to the complete set. The variety of shapes used to display the patterns ranged from biscuit barrels and tea caddies to candlesticks and vases.

Decorative themes were also diverse, from nursery rhymes and Kate Greenaway-style drawings, to Dickens' characters, contemporary cartoons and all-over floral motifs. Present-day collectors choose to seek out either a certain shape, such as jugs, or to collect items compatible by illustration such as Blue Children or Canterbury Pilgrims.

In the past there have been many memorable Series Ware plates. One of the most popular in 1900 was produced by a collaboration between Royal Doulton and the talented American artist Charles Dana Gibson. The Gibson Girls were drawn in fine black ink on a white background, the 10-inch plates were then finished with a wide cobalt blue border of stylised foliage. The drawings followed the exploits of the beautiful, Edwardian, Gibson girls who were seen as the personification of American womanhood. The first of the series featured the rather poignant but entertaining tale of *A Widow and Her Friends*. The twenty-four scenes followed a young woman's grief over the death of her loved one.

Cups and saucers are as popular with collectors as plates. They are linked by shape or themes such as flowers, colours and months, some are ornately decorated with 22-carat gold borders and displayed in glass fronted cabinets and units.

Dressing table or toilet sets as they were known, are still popular today in Royal Doulton's giftware ranges. Earlier series would have been centred around a large basin and jug, known as a ewer, equivalent to our handbasins for washing because in those days hot and cold running water was not widely available. Other items in the range included a puff box and pomade box. These days Royal Doulton offer an extensive range of giftware. Fine bone china trinket boxes, powder bowls, hairbrush trays, ginger jars and vases are available in a variety of designs such as Camilla, Arabella and Mystic Dawn. There's also a collection called

One way of forming a collection is to concentrate on one shape and to search for designs on this shape. Here are six different Series Ware designs on three ewer and bowl shapes, 'Lagoon', 'Lowther' and 'Mayfair'. Catalogue page c1924.

Sleighride which, as the name indicates, has a Christmas theme. The shapes and patterns are designed to be complementary to the interior design and colour schemes of contemporary homes. Giftware also includes bowls, vases and other decorative accessories in popular tableware patterns such as Real Old Willow, so that a co-ordinated look can be achieved with tea and dinner services.

Decorated picture plates, often referred to as rack plates, have been in production since Series Ware was launched. Rack plates are so called because traditionally they were displayed on a thin rack or rail around the top portion of the walls of a room, similar to a picture rail. Royal Doulton produce seasonal series for events such as Christmas and Valentine's day. Christmas Carols were the theme for a set of plates launched in 1983; they included Silent Night and the popular I Saw Three Ships. The latter was illustrated with a rosy-cheeked boy snugly dressed in his duffle coat with a woolly scarf and Tam o'Shanter hat, watching three fishing boats come into harbour. From 1989 to 1992 the theme for a series of four Christmas plates was Family Christmas. The finely detailed pictures showed all the warmth and charm of family gatherings at that special occasion. The 1992 plate depicted Going to Church, with a family walking up a snow-covered path to an old, stone church; the two younger children are following behind on a sledge. Designer Neil Faulkner used his own family experiences as inspiration for these appealing Christmas paintings.

Neil Faulkner painting the original design for the Faulkner Collection of plates depicting Royal Doulton figures in appropriate settings. This is 'Gail'.

Tea pots decorated with various Series Ware designs, c1925.

A collection of Bunnykins nurseryware shapes and design from c1950 to the present day.

All these plates were given their own individual "PN" number. Like the HN numbers on figures and the D numbers on Character Jugs, the PN number provides the collector with a unique reference to any plate in the range.

The most prestigious of the new collections was undoubtedly the Kings and Queens of the Realm series, and in recognition of the importance of this collection, it was given the honour of carrying the first four of the new Royal Doulton plate numbers. Many months were spent in locating an artist capable of doing full justice to the subject matter of the series, before the commission was given to leading Spanish artist Jose Miralles. Further time was spent in careful research to ensure the historical accuracy of the persons and scenes depicted. The first plate in the series, Queen Elizabeth I Knighting Sir Francis Drake (PN1) demonstrates eloquently the skill which he brought to this work.

Whereas most collectors' plates measure around 8 inches, the Kings and Queens of the Realm collection features bone china plates a full 10 inches in diameter, allowing justice to be done to the colour and detail of the original artwork. The border of each plate incorporates heraldic emblems from the arms of the monarch depicted, and has been developed in collaboration with the Royal College of Arms. Each plate in the collection was issued in a limited edition of 3,500 pieces, individually numbered and accompanied by a certificate of authenticity. The other three plates in the collection were issued at six-monthly intervals, depicting King Henry VIII with Anne Boleyn (PN2), the Coronation of Queen Victoria (PN3) and King Henry V at the Battle of Agincourt (PN4).

The second new collection in the Collectors Gallery had a very different, but equally popular appeal. In a limited edition of 3,500 of each, the Classic Florals collection comprised four 9-inch plates depicting colourful arrangements of beautiful flowers by Albert Williams, one of Britain's most recognised still life artists.

Staffordshire-born artist Anthony Forster has a long-standing association with Royal Doulton, having once worked in the Flambé department at the Nile Street factory. His Village Life collection, first introduced in 1989, proved very popular with collectors, and in response to demand four new subjects were introduced in 1993. Although not part of the Collectors Gallery, Gentle Persuasion (PN9), Water's Edge (PN10), The Village in the Vale (PN11) and Homeward Bound (PN12) were inspired by the landscape of the heart of Britain and capture the flavour of a nostalgic, peaceful era not so long ago.

The development of a new series of collectors' plates is a long, painstaking process. It is rare for a concept to be transformed into a finished plate in under twelve months. One of the most difficult tasks which face a product development team is the location of the right artist. The circular format of a ceramic plate requires a different discipline from the normal square or rectangular shape dictated by a picture frame, and many talented artists have found great difficulty in adapting to its demands. Modifying existing artwork for use on a plate is rarely successful, for important details in the corner of a painting may be lost, or the focus of the composition distorted.

Once an artist has been found whose work is suitable for the plate medium, who cannot only do justice to the subject but can also bring his or her own unique inspiration to the

project, the work is only just beginning. It may take several months before the painting is completed to the satisfaction of both the artist and Royal Doulton. Once the original artwork has been approved, it is passed onto a specialist lithograph company, where the time-consuming business of transforming the artist's work into a colour transfer for reproduction begins.

Unlike general printing, which uses only four electronically separated primary colours, ceramic printing requires every individual colour in a design to be isolated by a skilful combination of photographic and hand-worked separations. This is a very specialised and time-consuming process and many of the artists who do this work undergo an apprenticeship of several years to learn their trade. This colour separation work is of particular importance for collectors' plates as the original artwork has to be matched exactly and for this reason up to twenty-five individual colours may be used.

When each colour has been separated, the artwork is photographed, broken down into very small dots and printed to within extremely fine tolerances on special gummed paper. The finished transfer is then coated with a special lacquer cover which allows the design to be transferred from the paper onto the bone china plate. Once dry, the plate is fired at over 800°C, at which temperature the lacquer cover burns away and the special ceramic colours reveal their true brilliance.

Even after all this patient, careful work, it is possible that the first proof of the transfer might not be entirely

Plate issued to commemorate the 75th Anniversary of the Royal Air Force, designed by Geoff Hunt. Available as a limited edition of 14,750 through Lawleys by Post.

A collection of figures and shapes from The Snowman collection, after Raymond Briggs. The Snowman series was introduced in 1985.

A special limited edition colourway of Bunnykins Royal Family commissioned by UK International Ceramics in 1990.

Left to right: Ace Bunnykins (1896-1989); Uncle Sam Bunnykins (introduced in USA in 1986); Home Run Bunnykins (introduced in 1986). All by David Lyttleton after Harry Sales.

satisfactory. Occasionally more work, involving the creation of one or more additional proofs and a period of several months, is required before the colour reproduction matches the original artwork to everyone's satisfaction. Although photo-electronics have speeded up this process in recent years, it is still highly dependent upon the skills of the artist and the printer to ensure that the finished transfer is of the standard demanded by Royal Doulton and, ultimately, the discerning collector.

An important aspect of any plate to a serious collector, ranking behind only the artist and the subject, is the backstamp. As a result of collector interest, the backstamps of collectors' plates have become crammed with more and more information, such as details of the artist and background on the scene depicted. Collectors' plates feature the signature of the artist and the plate's individual PN number. Limited editions include the plate's individual number, added by hand, while many series feature additional details, such as the charming descriptions of times gone by which can be found on the back of the Village Life collection.

NURSERYWARE

Nurserywares are very special to Royal Doulton because we have our own unique characters, called Bunnykins. Bunnykins was created and originally drawn by a nun, Barbara Vernon, who was also the daughter of Cuthbert

Below: Billy Bunnykins (Charles Noke, 1939-c1944). Astro Bunnykins ('Rocket Man', David Lyttleton after Harry Sales, 1983-1988).

Above and Below: Designs for the 'Toy Shop', showing the original design and how it was reversed before being put into production, Walter Hayward after Barbara Vernon, 1959-1967.

Bunnykins design by Colin Twinn.

A Teddy Bear Tea Party using Brambly Hedge tea wares.

Bailey, general manager of Royal Doulton from 1925. Although Bunnykins is sixty years old, it is still an immensely popular range, both in tableware and figure models. Characters such as Santa Bunnykins, Bedtime and Storytime are favourites with collectors.

Also of importance to us is the production under licence, of characters made popular through books or films, such as *Brambly Hedge* and *The Snowman*. Royal Doulton produce a wide range of tableware, giftware and figures based on the characters and adventures portrayed in these books. A number of manufacturers offer children's mugs, bowls and plates made in plastic and decorated with violent cartoon figures whose speech bubbles shriek 'Wham' and 'Pow'. In contrast to such aggressively decorated products Royal Doulton offer traditional style, quality, china nurserywares.

The charm of children's ware is that the subject involved, such as the mice of *Brambly Hedge* and the characters of *The Snowman*, convey their tales and stories by action and expression. The antics of the Bunnykins bunnies are portrayed in model or picture form with little or no writing, so they are easily understood by children from an early age and of any nationality. My brother and I were both brought up with Bunnykins tableware and, being the age that I am, the illustrations on our plates and mugs were probably from the original drawings by Barbara Vernon. The next generation of my family have also followed in the Bunnykins tradition; my young stepdaughter Sacha now has her own collection of the more recent designs including the Brownie figure which is proudly displayed on the shelf in her bedroom.

Brambly Hedge plates from the Interiors collection. Left to right: Store Stump, The Dairy, Crabapple Cottage and Old Oak Palace.

Bunnykins commissions for the Royal Doulton International Collectors Club. Left to right: Bunny's Bedtime (HN3370, Nada Pedley, limited edition of 9,500, 1991); Collector Bunnykins, David Lyttleton, 1987); Master Potter Bunnykins (Warren Platt, 1992).

Bunnykins creator, Barbara Vernon, joined an English convent and became a nun, known as Sister Mary Barbara. She started drawing the mischievous little bunnies in letters to friends and younger members of her family. Her father, Cuthbert Bailey, took the drawings to the factory and had them adapted for production by designer Hubert Light. Lithograph designs were then prepared to decorate china. The first Bunnykins beakers, mugs and plates were launched in 1934. During the first five years Bunnykins appeared only on tableware and other functional items such as nightlights and hot water plates. It was not until 1939 that the first Bunnykins figures appeared; they were Billy, Mary, Reggie, Farmer complete with smocked overall and knotted handkerchief parcel and Mother Bunnykins with a baby bunny snoozing on her lap. These figures are now very rare and are highly prized by collectors.

Over 100 different Bunnykins figures have been produced since then. The models, approximately 4 inches high have followed various pursuits and celebrate any number of important events. There have been Freefall Bunnykins landing on his bottom after a parachute jump, Ace Bunnykins looking as though he would frighten even Monica Seles at Wimbledon and a fit-looking Jogging Bunnykins. Special models have been made for events such as the Olympics – the figure for this occasion is portrayed in shorts and singlet carrying the Olympic torch. In 1990 a special edition of the Bunnykins Oompah Band, renamed the Royal Doulton Collectors Band, was made for UK International Ceramics. The Band became the centrepiece of the UK Doulton Fair in London. This limited edition of five, smartly-uniformed band members – Drum Major, Cymbals, Sousaphone, Trumpeter and Drummer complete with big bass drum – are now very collectable. We have also produced special figures for the North American market – such as Magician Bunnykins and Halloween Bunnykins.

The product ranges have also expanded from china tableware, figures and giftware to stationery, shopping bags, aprons and books. Today the future of Bunnykins is in the capable hands of Graham Tongue and his team. Warren Platt has modelled many of the subjects in recent years.

In 1991 Bunnykins inspired a very special figure called Bunny's Bedtime (HN3370). The exclusive 6-inch figure, in a limited edition of 9500, was modelled by Nada Pedley for the Royal Doulton International Collectors Club. Bunny's Bedtime portrays a little girl with her hair tied in bunches. The little girl appears to be on her way to bed wearing a blue *broderie anglaise* nightdress with toy bunny tucked closely under one arm and Bunnykins mug, complete with tiny pattern, in the other hand. The Bunnykins mug, which is no larger than a fingertip, is decorated with an early Barbara Vernon illustration, accurately recreated in miniature.

Two Nurseryware designs. Left, plate, cup and saucer depicting scenes from Alice in Wonderland. *Right, plate, teapot, jug, cup and saucer, Nursery Rhymes by William Savage Cooper, 1903 to c1940. Queen Alexandra ordered this nursery design for use by her grandchildren.*

Another of our current ranges, Brambly Hedge, has been in production since 1982 when Royal Doulton acquired the right to reproduce the figures from Jill Barklem's stories about a family of mice. Each design that Royal Doulton creates has to be approved by Jill so that the charm and vitality of the figures can be ensured. Jill's *Four Seasons* books, first published in 1980, have been reprinted twenty-eight times, and translated into twelve languages with nearly two million copies in print worldwide. The Brambly Hedge collection, featuring the daily life and antics of such popular characters as Wilfred Toadflax and Primrose Woodmouse in the flowering hedgerow home, can be found on a wide range of pieces. Wall plates, miniatures, tea and breakfast sets and bedroom accessories are all decorated with the Brambly Hedge theme.

The tableware sets and wallplates seem to be as popular with adult collectors as they are with younger ones. The character figures have an ageless appeal, especially with their flowery connections and names.

The Snowman is also produced under licence and is taken directly from the appealing story by Raymond Briggs. The antics of the young boy James and his magical Snowman friend are portrayed on tableware and in model form. The Snowman appears in many guises such as a Drummer and Highlander, the latter showing a Snowman doing the highstepping fling in a smart tartan kilt and sporran. The Snowman is popular all year round but really comes into his own at Christmas time.

The Snowman also holds special memories for me. A few years ago we decided, for promotional purposes, that we would make a costume of The Snowman. A member of staff was to dress up in the costume and be on hand at store

The Twins, designed by John Hassall. Illustrated are examples of two vases, the one on the right copying the drawing to the story by Edward Shirley.

events, especially at Christmas time. During a visit to eastern Canada, where it was particularly cold and snowing at the time, we were invited to dinner at the home of one of our customers. As a joke, I decided to put on The Snowman costume. I walked up to the front door of his house, in about two feet of snow, and rang the doorbell. The door was opened by the family with their two very large dogs at their side. The dogs took one look at me and jumped, forcing me to the ground. Luckily the suit was well padded and I came to no harm, but the family were so overcome with laughter that it took them some time before they could help me to my feet again.

Our nurseryware ranges continue to expand today and Bunnykins has passed through a number of careful creators. Sister Mary Barbara soon relinquished responsibility for Bunnykins and the drawing of the bunny tales was passed on to Royal Doulton artist Hubert Light. After the Second World War, Walter Hayward, later an Art Director at Royal Doulton, took over the task of creating new Bunnykins adventures. He continued to follow Barbara's lead, but added his own cheeky little mice to some of the bunnies' escapades. The designs also became more complicated under Walter's supervision and contemporary life was reflected, for example Bunnykins were depicted watching television! Many of his designs are still in production today.

In 1988 Colin Twinn, a well known illustrator of children's books, took on the task of illustrating a new series of books about the Bunnykins family, published by Frederick Warne. A number of Colin's illustrations have been used on Bunnykins nurseryware and as inspiration for new figures. His work is now used for special commissions and projects.

Housed at the Sir Henry Doulton Gallery are the Bunnykins Archives. These comprise early catalogues, a photocopy of an original story by Barbara Vernon, an album of watercolours painted by Walter Hayward and a third book contains lithographs of the finished designs as used in production.

Royal Doulton's connection with nurserywares pre-dates the appearance of Bunnykins and goes back to the nineteenth century. The original Doulton works at Lambeth produced cot-size stoneware hot water bottles inscribed with the word 'Baby'. There were also filters and feeding bottles. However, the real development and interest in nurseryware can be traced back to Victorian times when there was a growing awareness and recognition of the specific needs of children. Until this time children had been treated as miniature adults.

Poor children suffered desperate conditions, being sent to work down mines, in factories, and as chimney sweeps. Following a number of Parliamentary Acts, children became legally protected. The Factory Reform Act of 1833 barred children under nine years of age from all textile factories and the hours of older children were limited to a maximum of forty-eight hours a week. It was also stated that every factory child should have two hours schooling a day. Various health and education acts of the 1870s finally established that adults had a specific responsibility for the young.

Children's clothing was a small version of adults' clothes, with restricting petticoats, tightly laced, heeled boots and tailored jackets. The more enlightened attitude towards children saw their clothing become looser and more practical, giving them freedom of movement and comfort. Children's clothing was an important feature of the delightful illustrations by the artist Kate Greenaway. Her children are dressed in the style of the 'Aesthetic' period of the 1880s and 90s. Little girls are shown in high-waisted frocks falling from a yoke neckline, worn with a bonnet or 'Tammy' – a far cry from the dungarees and trainers of today. Kate Greenaway's illustrations were later used to decorate a number of Series Ware items and the illustrator herself was dubbed 'Queen of the Nursery'.

Another illustrator of that period, whose work subsequently appeared on several ranges of Royal Doulton Series Ware, was Randolph Caldecott. His illustrations of nursery rhymes such as 'My Pretty Maid' were transferred onto china and were very popular. His home at 46 Great Russell Street, opposite the British Museum, is marked by a blue ceramic commemorative plaque made by Royal Doulton.

The style of decoration and illustrations in children's books and pictures also changed. The moralistic verses such as 'Children should be seen and not heard' were abandoned in favour of more fanciful and enjoyable nursery rhymes and fairy tales. Such changes brought new openings for toy manufacturers, book publishers and of course Royal Doulton. Charles Noke recognised the opportunities in this market and realised the potential for china specifically designed for children.

Early Royal Doulton nurseryware dates from 1884 and came from the Pinder and Bourne factory that Sir Henry Doulton took over. Two of the early designs, Le Mouchoir Retrouve and Bonjour M'sieur le Marquis, remained in production until 1913. However, the real expansion of the nurseryware business started with the Nursery Rhyme range Charles Noke supervised. Forty-seven rhymes in fifteen different series have been recorded. Other designs were based on well-known children's stories such as *Alice's Adventures in Wonderland* and *Through the Looking Glass* both by Lewis Carroll.

One of Noke's most successful collaborations was with William Savage Cooper, a fine artist who exhibited his paintings at the Royal Academy. The nursery rhyme designs Savage Cooper created for Royal Doulton in 1903 were still

A collection of figures with a child theme. Left to right: Sophie (HN2833), Peggy Davies, 1977 to 1987, Kate Greenaway series; Boy Evacuee (HN3202, Lawleys-by-Post exclusive, Adrian Hughes, introduced in 1988); James (HN3013, Pauline Parsons, 1983 to 1987, Kate Greenaway series); A Child's Grace (HN62A, L. Perugini, 1916 to 1938); Little Boy Blue (HN3035, Adrian Hughes, 1984 to 1987).

Three figures depicting children, the first two modelled by Adrian Hughes and commissioned by Lawleys-by-Post in a limited edition of 9,500. Daddy's Joy (HN3294, 1990); Santa's Helper (HN3301, 1991); Feeding Time (HN3373, Nada Pedley, introduced in 1991).

so popular in the 1930s that a new earthernware range was launched. Amongst Savage Cooper's designs was one based on the nursery rhyme 'Hey Diddle Diddle'. The lines he chose to illustrate included 'The cow jumped over the moon' and 'The dish ran away with the spoon'. HM Queen Alexandra (the wife of King Edward VII) was so taken by his charming illustrations that she ordered the nurseryware for use by her grandchildren – a royal seal of approval that further increased its popularity. In 1905 a forty-piece teaset – obviously for a large nursery of children – was advertised for £1.10 shillings (now £1.50p).

In the early 1900s Royal Doulton also collaborated with the famous poster artist and book illustrator John Hassall. His best-known works include the 'Skegness is So Bracing' railway poster and advertising illustrations for Colman's mustard. Lithographs from Hassall's illustrations of 'The Twins' appeared on numerous Lambeth stoneware shapes such as jugs, jardinières and vases. 'The Twins' tales extolled the virtues of the good brother and condemned the antics of the bad brother. The brothers are introduced in the following poem:

Paul Montgomery Vincent Green
Was the very best boy that ever was seen
He had a twin brother, and strange to say
This brother was born on the very same day.

Peter Augustus Marmaduke Green
Was the very worst boy that ever was seen
He had a twin brother, and strange to rehearse,
I've mentioned his name in the very first verse.

On one tall jug the mischievous Peter can be seen in his nightshirt, standing on a stack of books and reaching into a larder. The caption for this tale reads 'He went exploring round and round. A cupboard full of jam he found'.

Between 1914 and 1917 a number of child figure studies were made including Shy Anne (HN60), The Little Land (HN63) and A Child's Grace (HN62). Child studies are still popular today, and figures such as Children of the Blitz, a pair made up of Boy Evacuee (HN3202) and Girl Evacuee (HN3203), issued in 1989 to commemorate the wartime evacuation in 1939, capture the sorrowful plight of young children sent from the cities to live with families in the relative safety of the countryside.

Royal Doulton's connections with the nursery go still further. There are a number of figures such as Sophie (HN2833) and Emma (HN2834) from the Kate Greenaway series, modelled by Peggy Davies in 1977 and 1981. There are other figures such as Mary Mary (HN2044), She Loves

Me Not (HN2045), He Loves Me (HN2046) and Once Upon A Time (HN2047) all designed by the modeller Leslie Harradine in 1949. Mary, Mary was the last of this popular range to be withdrawn, in 1973. Peggy Davies also modelled Wee Willie Winkie (HN2050), Mary Had a Little Lamb (HN2048) and Curly Locks (HN2049) at the same time as Harradine. On a visit to the factory in 1984 The Princess of Wales was invited to cast the nursery rhyme figure of Little Boy Blue (HN3035), which was then sent to her own young son Prince William.

More recent Child Study figures include Little Ballerina (HN3395) and Ballet Shoes (HN3434). Both of these charming studies were modelled by Alan Maslankowski. Santa's Helper (HN3301) modelled by Adrian Hughes portrays a child struggling with a sack full of seasonal gifts.

Right: Sweetheart Bunnykins (Warren Platt, introduced in the USA in 1992).

Little Ballerina (HN3395, Alan Maslankowski, introduced in 1992).

The charming Dressing Up (HN3300) also by Adrian portrays a little girl wearing a hat, dress and shoes, several sizes too big for her. Bedtime (HN3418) by Nada Pedley, depicts a small girl in her dressing gown with teddy and book, on her way to bed. These recent figures are typical of the continuing tradition of child figures.

In the early 1900s, the Company produced a number of Nursery Rhyme and Fairy Tale ceramic tile panels for children's wards in hospitals. The Victorians' concern for child health saw the opening of several specialist hospitals and wards. The wards were normally tiled throughout for hygenic reasons, often in clinical white and green. Royal Doulton's artists created the pictorial panels to brighten up the monotonous surroundings for the young patients. The panels were usually about 5 feet high and between 2 feet and 5 feet wide and were made in pairs or series from familiar tales such as Little Red Riding Hood, Cinderella and Little Boy Blue.

To create these panels was a complex and difficult job. A full-scale painting was drawn up from the artist's original work. A team of faience painters then carefully copied from the squared-off, full-scale drawing onto the individual tiles. The decorated tiles were numbered on the reverse side and fired, then transported to the final location and assembled.

One of the best known exponents of tile painting was John McLennan, who also executed tile commissions for the King of Spain and the Tsar of Russia. Other well-known Lambeth artists to work on the hospital panels included Margaret Thompson who had a stylised approach to

painting, reminiscent of the Kate Greenaway style of illustration. Another artist, William Rowe, was also responsible for the largest panels ever made at the Lambeth studio. The panel was 23 feet high and consisted of over 8000 tiles for Singapore's terminal railway station.

The Lilian Ward at St Thomas's Hospital in south London, not far from the original Lambeth factory, is believed to have the first of the Royal Doulton tile schemes. The scheme for the ward was started in 1899 and finally, officially opened in 1901. St Thomas's Hospital has recently transferred sites but a number of their original panels line the corridors of a modern wing. Some of the old tile panels survived under layers of paint, but others were taken down and sold. One scenario, depicting Old King Cole, was removed from the old Seymour Ward and sold in 1970. Since then the pictorial panels have become much sought-after by collectors and the trustees of St Thomas's worked hard to raise funds and to track down the missing panel. It has since been reinstated at the hospital.

On 12 May 1990 the Royal Doulton Nursery Rhyme and Fairy Tale panels at St Thomas's Hospital were 'brought to life' to celebrate Florence Nightingale's birthday. The young patients in the children's wards were thrilled by the magical appearance of Sleeping Beauty, Little Red Riding Hood, Cinderella, Little Bo Peep and other favourites accompanied by Miss Nightingale complete in her crinoline skirt and lace-edged bonnet. The staff had dressed in costumes matching those on the panels.

Fairies at the Christening Tile Panel, Margaret Thompson, 1908. (Courtesy of Phillips).

The outbreak of the First World War brought a decline in the manufacturing of these decorative panels. Amongst the hospitals to receive the panels were University College Hospital in London, the Buchanan Hospital in Hastings, The Royal Hospital, Portsmouth and the Royal Victoria Infirmary in Newcastle-upon-Tyne. Some of these buildings still have panels, others have been relocated or cut down and sold to private collections. Unfortunately the cost of repairing and rescuing the panels is a costly business running up bills of thousands of pounds. These days hospital administrators feel that funds could be used more effectively on life-saving equipment, so restoration is usually left to the purses of private benefactors.

Panels similar to those at St Thomas's Hospital were made in 1910 for the Wellington Hospital in New Zealand. There were originally seventeen hand-painted murals depicting such rhymes as See-Saw Margery Daw. The tiles were put in storage in 1989 after the children's ward at the hospital was demolished and a fund-raising scheme was launched to collect around $150,000 for the panels to be re-sited. Part of the fund-raising involved two of the massive, concrete-backed panels being put on display in the Trust Bank in Wellington and The Oaks branch of the Trust Bank. Royal Doulton also launched a series of Nursery Rhyme plates in 1986 to help raise money for the rescue of the tile murals at Wellington Hospital. The four plates were painted by Neil Faulkner from the original panels; they were See-Saw Margery Daw, Little Bo-Peep, Little Boy Blue and Nuts an' May.

Perhaps one of the most unusual and far flung locations for our panels is the Sassoon Hospital in Poona. Angus Lindsay, a visitor to the hospital in 1981, reported that 'On the walls of the ENT ward there were eleven panels illustrating nursery rhymes and fairy tales, all signed by M.E. Thompson, Doulton & Co. Ltd, Lambeth, SE. Though badly disfigured by paint, the panels were all intact and complete. Six panels represent nursery-rhyme subjects and five are devoted to fairy tales, either rectangular or square tiles being used.'

In our family collection we had some early nurseryware pieces. I can remember as a child playing with a collection of little figures, my favourite being a big frog with a bat. My brother and I used to play games with the figures and many were damaged or destroyed. We didn't pay any special attention to them at the time, but now I know these were the figures modelled by George Tinworth and I wish we'd been a little more careful with them. Another childhood memory is of a series of cat-shaped door stops. I can still recall, quite vividly, the horror I felt when I accidentally kicked the tail off one of these cats. They were, I think, the work of one of the last Lambeth potters, Agnete Hoy.

It is remarkable how many of our adult collectors unwittingly started their Royal Doulton collections in childhood. It isn't until I ask them, or point out that their infant tableware carried our backstamp, that they realise their connection with the Company has been lifelong.

'The Football Scrimmage' (George Tinworth, C1885 to 1887). Michael played with frog models such as these as a child.

Gift of Life (HN3536, Russell Willis, introduced in 1987, from the Images of Fire collection).

Chapter 6
ART WARES

For over 150 years Royal Doulton's development has been influenced by the saying that our work is the 'Marriage of Art and Industry'. The Company combines the skills and artistic talents of individual modellers and decorators with the efficiency and quality that can be obtained through industrial organisation. This marriage of Art and Industry has resulted in some of the finest quality china produced today. Our products are sold throughout the world and the Royal Doulton backstamp has earned a reputation as a sign of excellence and style. We currently create works of art from the finest figures to gold-edged tableware and from life-like animal models to baby-size beakers. But our present success owes a sizeable debt to the past.

It was under Sir Henry Doulton's guidance that the foundations of the Company we know today were laid. Henry developed his father's business from an industrial concern making drainpipes, chimney pots, ridge tiles and garden vases into a highly respected manufacturer of fine art ware. His principle, upheld at both the Lambeth and Burslem studios, was that 'To distinguish between eccentricity and genius may be difficult but it is surely better to bear with singularity than to crush originality'. Henry Doulton's encouragement of such a philosophy and his natural flair for predicting new trends kept the Company in the forefront of developments. Amongst Henry Doulton's other abilities was a knack for recognising talent in other people and this perceptiveness was a vital factor in Royal Doulton's continuing development.

Henry Doulton's talents were noted elsewhere. In 1885 The Prince of Wales (later King Edward Vll) presented the potter with the Albert Medal of the Society of Arts. This was a rare and prestigious award, as only one was presented each year and others who received it included the internationally renowned scientist Louis Pasteur and the eminent botanist Joseph Hooker. The Prince also took the unusual step of presenting the award to Henry Doulton at the factory in Lambeth rather than at Marlborough House where such events usually took place. Sir Henry was always most adamant that the great honours bestowed upon him were not his alone. He readily admitted that the honours also belonged to those who worked in his Company, to the craftsmen and women, potters and painters who produced the ware both fanciful and plain, that bore the Doulton backstamp.

In the book *Sir Henry Doulton – The Man of Business as a Man of Imagination* by Edmund Gosse, edited by

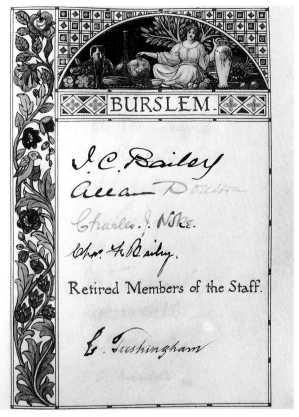

Illustration from a book presented to Henry Lewis Doulton to mark 25 years as Chairman. The book is signed by representatives at all the factories and departments. Illustrations by Arthur E. Pearce with lettering by William Rowe.

Desmond Eyles, is a description of the dedication and presentation of this honour. 'In June the Albert Medal was duly awarded to Henry Doulton, and The Prince of Wales consented to present it. In announcing their decision, the Council of the Society of Arts remarked that they "felt that the establishment of the new industry of artistic stoneware fully justified" the award.' The Council added a notable comment to the dedication, which highlighted Henry Doulton's philanthropic credits. 'While recording this opinion', the script continued, 'they wished it to be understood that in making the award they had also in view the other services rendered by Mr Doulton to the cause of technical education, especially the technical education of women, to sanitary science by the productions of his firm, and, though, in a less degree, to other branches of science by the manufacture of appliances of suitable character.'

Two years later Henry Doulton received a knighthood from Queen Victoria; he was the first potter to receive such an award and it was given in recognition of his services to the pottery industry. The elaborately embellished citation for this knighthood hangs in a gilded frame in the hallway of my mother's house. I have walked past it thousands of times in my life but still feel proud of my ancestor's achievements. In 1901, the first year of King Edward VII's reign, the King bestowed another honour on the Doulton Company. The King presented the Chairman with a Royal Warrant of Appointment and, at the same time, authorised the use of the word 'Royal' to describe the Company's products. This is a rare distinction and quite separate from the warrant itself. From this date the Company became known as 'Royal Doulton'.

Collection of vases produced in the art studios, Lambeth, showing the different techniques developed there. Left to right: Vase, Silicon Ware, designed by Eliza Simmance, 1884; Vase, Doulton Ware, designed by Frank Butler, 1906; Vase, Chiné Ware, 1902; Inkwell, 'Votes for Women' in salt-glazed stoneware, designed by Leslie Harradine, c1905; Inkwell, Leatherware, in imitation of a cricket ball, modeller unknown, c1882.

Portrait of Edward VII, painted by George White to commemorate the granting of the Royal Warrant to the Company by the King and the specific right to use the title "Royal", c1902.

Sir Henry was also a generous benefactor. Many buildings have received donations of decorative tiles and terracotta building materials from the Doulton Company. In 1884 The Princess of Wales, later Queen Alexandra, laid the foundation stone for a house to be named after her. The house provided a suitable home for young ladies studying art, music and science in London. Sir Henry, well-known for his support of working women and whose own art studios were staffed mainly by women, provided some exceptional tiling for Queen Alexandra's House. Faience mantlepieces for all the principal rooms, a terracotta sculptural group for the entrance doorway and scenic view panels of the High Street Lambeth and Bishops Walk were provided free of charge or at cost price. Queen Alexandra's House continues today in its original function as a hostel for students and

many of the original Royal Doulton ceramics can be seen there.

H. Lewis Doulton carried on the firm's tradition for helping worthy causes. Amongst the still visible works are an elaborate Art Nouveau panel and the green tiles for the porchway of the Royal Hospital for Children and Women in Waterloo Road, London SE1. The Company also gave a nursey-rhyme tile panel for the children's ward inside, but this was recently removed and taken to the children's wing at the nearby St Thomas's Hospital. The Doulton Ward was named after our family in recognition of the many contributions made to St Thomas's Hospital and our links with the ward have continued through my father and myself. We still contribute china and other items towards Christmas festivities and the general day-to-day work of the ward.

I have recently been involved with the Florence Nightingale Museum which opened in the grounds of St Thomas's Hospital. Royal Doulton produced a special figure of Florence Nightingale (HN3144), modelled by Pauline Parsons. The founder of modern nursing, Miss Nightingale, is portrayed as a young lady in her early thirties wearing a green dress and burgundy shawl. On an ivy-clad column beside her is her pet owl Athena. The model was inspired by a sketch drawn by Florence's sister Parthenope. A limited edition of 5000 pieces was made and a substantial donation, over £17,250, from the sales of these figures was given to the Florence Nightingale Museum Trust. Amongst other functions the Trust awards bursaries to nurses for the futherance of the nursing profession.

Henry Doulton, the man who was rewarded by Royalty and fêted by nobility, had started his working life with his hands deep in clay. Henry had joined his father John in the pottery company when he was 15 years old. His father had recognised Henry's academic ability and encouraged him to pursue a career in politics or the church, but Henry was adamant that he would join the family firm. Henry sought no favours. He started as an apprentice and worked his way

Faience Jug with decoration of two young children in contemporary costume by Ada Dennis assisted by Josephine Durtnall and Gertrude Smith, Lambeth Art Studios, c1894.

pipe and charcoal filters he was given the opportunity to model and decorate a few vases. At the Paris Exhibition of 1867 Henry Doulton showed some of Tinworth's ornamental vases and pots. The response was encouraging.

At the International Exhibition in South Kensington in 1871 a display of Doulton's decorated stoneware drew a lot of comment and enquiries. That same year, having gauged his market, Henry Doulton founded the Lambeth Art Pottery studio. In contrast to his successful industrial business, artware did not prove immediately profitable, but Doulton had no regrets. He is said to have described the new business as 'one of the few sacrificial tributes of Commerce to Art'. As well as Tinworth, Doulton employed other artists such as Hannah Barlow, her brother Arthur and sisters Florence and Lucy (mentioned in Chapter 2). As the studio became established, new styles, techniques and glazes were developed.

Amongst the many innovative styles associated with Lambeth is Sgraffito. The studio developed their own version of the original German technique which produced a design by scratching or engraving through a coat of white slip (liquid clay). The light surface clay was applied over the darker, firmer clay of the pot underneath. The pattern was achieved by the contrast of the dark lines underneath being revealed through the lighter surface. Doulton showed their expanding Art Wares ranges at the Philadelphia Exhibition in 1876. The Company won five first-class awards and established a relationship with the North American market which continues to this day.

The Royal Doulton Company still follows in Sir Henry Doulton's steps, exhibiting at both domestic and international fairs. In 1992 our stand at EXPO in Seville

through the various stages until he qualified as a master potter. This apprenticeship gave him a valuable working knowledge of the craft and the pottery business.

By the time he was 30 years of age Henry was a driving force in the family firm and had become friends with John Sparkes, Principal of the Lambeth School of Art. Henry's appreciation of art and his enquiring mind led him to give one of Sparkes's young pupils, George Tinworth, a job at the pottery. Although Tinworth started his career making

A variety of pieces produced at the Lambeth and Burslem Studios between c1880 and c1950. Courtesy of Phillips.

showed the best of our contemporary ranges and included a special four-foot high model of a girl with her arms outstretched, holding a crystal. The figure, called 'Discovery', was modelled by Angela Munslow, a mature student at the Sir Henry Doulton School of Sculpture. (Further details of the Sculpture School are on page 117.)

Other new decorating techniques developed in the early days of the Lambeth Art Ware studio include *pâte-sur-pâte*. This was Doulton's own version of a technique introduced to England by a French artist called Louis Solon who came from Sèvres, the great French pottery region, in 1870. *Pâte-sur-pâte* is a delicate form of decoration in which several coats of semi-liquid coloured clay (slip) are applied by brush or pencil until they build up a raised design. Florence Barlow (Hannah's sister) became a master of this style of decoration, and her work is now very sought after. My wife Pruna and myself are lucky enough to have two fine vases in *pâte-sur-pâte*. They were decorated by Hannah Barlow with one of her favourite subjects, horses. The vases are placed on a sideboard at our house in Sussex and attract appreciative comments from both china enthusiasts and horse lovers alike.

Faience was also developed at the south London studio. This decoration was achieved by applying colour to a biscuit (once-fired) base. Designs had to be painted quickly because the porous biscuit body would absorb the colour – it must have been like painting on blotting paper. The paints used to create Faience ware were made from a mixture of metallic oxides and oil. In the heat of the kiln the colours of the metallic paints would change dramatically so the artists had to take these changes into consideration as they painted.

In 1880 there was a great surge of interest in Egypt. The Suez Canal was opened and new archaeological discoveries were being unearthed. The discovery of Giza during the 1870s resulted in both Liberty & Co. and Tiffany the jewellers producing objects inspired by Egyptian artefacts and style. The trend spread from Liberty's in Regent Street, as well as the couture fashion houses, to the Lambeth Studios where the new and only recently perfected Silicon decoration was used to produce Egyptian-style ornaments. Silicon Ware was decorated in various ways, a popular technique used a relief decoration which was cut out of clay and stuck to the surface of smooth, terracotta stoneware – a technique that my wife Pruna assures me is similar to the art of *appliqué* in needlework. The finished ornament was fired and usually left with a flat, no-gloss effect although some examples have been found with a dull eggshell finish known to potters as a 'smear'.

Another decorative technique at the Royal Doulton studios was created by the opposite effect. Natural Foliage, otherwise known as Repoussé ware, was created by pressing real leaves into the soft clay surface. Once an impression of the leaf had been made in the clay the leaf was carefully peeled away. The impression was then painted to represent a real leaf either in subtle autumnal shades or vital springtime greens. A similar technique was used to make Chiné Ware, but instead of pressing leaves into the clay, lace, linen and fine net were used to create fine textured patterns. Examples of Chiné Ware are keenly sought by collectors.

Repoussé Ware leaves may have looked almost real, but the ultimate 'lookalike' finish was achieved on copper and black leatherware developed in 1887. The jugs, tankards, tobacco jars and boxes were decorated as though made from real copper and leather. Rivets, stitches, dents and seams were all accurately reproduced onto the clay. Looking at

examples of this ware today, in the Sir Henry Doulton Gallery at Nile Street, I still find it hard to believe that the mugs and jugs are made of clay, not leather. You really have to pick up a piece and touch it before you are wholly convinced.

Another development from the studio was Crown Lambeth ware. This style showed just how fine and delicate decoration on earthenware could be. Colour was applied in stages, and fired after each layer of painting was completed. The result was a very subtle, soft blending of the shades but the numerous firings meant that many pieces were damaged or broken in the process. Consequently the few pieces that have survived to this day fetch high prices at auction. There is a family story that suggests that Sir Henry was advised by his accountants to stop making Crown Lambeth ware, because so many pieces were ruined in the kiln. Always a man to know his own mind, Sir Henry dismissed their advice and the production of Crown Lambeth Artwares continued.

Perhaps some of the best known and easily viewed work from the Lambeth Studio, was that created in terracotta. The unglazed buff and orange-coloured clay was originally used for the chimney pots and building wares that Henry's father John had produced at the factory. But under Henry's imaginative guidance the practical terracotta clay was transformed into an artist's medium. One of the great masters of terracotta modelling was Henry's protégé George Tinworth. Tinworth created a number of exceptional, biblically inspired works. Queen Victoria was so impressed with one of his religious tableaux that she ordered it to be sent to Windsor Castle.

Decorative, architectural terracotta panels were used on the façades of buildings and many can still be seen today. In London, Harrods department store in Knightsbridge, The Savoy hotel on The Strand, Harrow School and several hotels and buildings in Russell Square can all be easily viewed from street level. Woollpits House in Surrey, once a Doulton family home built by Sir Henry, is now a school but still retains many fine examples of Doulton terracotta decoration. At my mother's home there is a large decorative terracotta panel depicting animals, which was incorporated into a front porch extension that my father had built.

Commissions were also received from overseas, for example from the Canadian Pacific Railroad Hotel in Vancouver. The offices of the *Calgary Herald* were decorated with caricatures of newspaper staff by Mark Marshall. Other countries where Doulton terracotta was used include India, Mexico and South Africa.

In the early 1900s the Lambeth Pottery began to decline and the majority of the business was transferred to the new establishment that Sir Henry had set up in Burslem in Staffordshire. By 1914 most of the leading artists whose work had made the Lambeth Pottery such a prestigious place, had retired or died. However, talented artists continued to work in the studios including Harry Simeon, Vera Huggins and William Rowe. From 1937 to 1939 a young potter called Joan Cowper based herself at the south London studios. She produced hand-thrown pots and vases decorated in contemporary styles. During the Second World War Royal Doulton turned production over to making laboratory and technical porcelain for the war effort. For the final four years, from 1952 until Lambeth finally closed in 1956, Agnete Hoy from Copenhagen Art School made stoneware at Lambeth. She produced the last piece of

Sculptures from the façade of the offices of the Calgary Herald, Calgary, Canada, modelled by Mark Marshall.

Two Doulton Persian Ware vases designed by William Rowe, c1925 and 'Reaper', modelled by Leslie Harradine, c1910.

The Art Studios, Lambeth, closed in 1956. The vase on the left was the last piece to be made. The cat on the right was one of twelve modelled by Agnete Hoy in c1956.

pottery to be fired in the historic kilns. The vogue for decorated stoneware declined throughout the twentieth century to be replaced by the finer and more delicate artistry associated with fine china.

I remember my father talking, with sadness in his voice, about the closure of the Lambeth factory. I think he felt that it was a shame to stop all production at the site where the Company was founded. He put forward the idea that a token amount of production should be carried on at the London factory, as it would be of interest to overseas visitors. He also felt that the considerable acreage of the site at Lambeth should not be sold at that time, as the market was not good. In hindsight he may have been right as land on the south bank of the Thames now fetches premium prices.

With the closure of the Lambeth factory Royal Doulton transferred all its manufacturing and decorating work to Stoke-on-Trent. The Company is now concentrated in and around the site of Sir Henry's Stoke-on-Trent business. Having established the Lambeth Art Studios, Henry looked further afield to expand his burgeoning business. In 1877 he entered a partnership and in 1882 bought a medium-sized, middle-of-the-road earthenware factory called Pinder & Bourne Company in Nile Street, Burslem. The legacy of Lambeth Artware, experiments with paint effects and finishes was carried on and developed at this new Royal Doulton premises in Stoke-on-Trent. Burslem is a small town in the heart of North Staffordshire and is known locally as the 'Mother Town'. At first the local potters did not welcome the interloper from London and Henry's innovative and unconventional ideas soon caused a stir.

From the original Pinder & Bourne Company staff Henry appointed a young decorating manager called John Slater to take control of his new Company. Henry is said to have instructed Slater to 'Forget, for heaven's sake, most of what was done here in the past. We are going to make a new

beginning and I intend, come what may, to bring the products up to the standards we have set ourselves in Lambeth.' Another shock came with his appointment of 23-year-old John Cuthbert Bailey as general manager of the Company. But Henry's faith in these young men was proven right. They brought not only style and art to their work but also developed an organisation and production system which took the Company into the twentieth century.

Slater recruited artists and craftsmen from local art and design schools, and he also spent time inventing and developing new techniques. It was Slater who perfected the system of transferring photographic images onto pottery, a forerunner of the lithographic transfers we use today. This process provided outlines for hand-painting and transferred photographs onto commemorative wares or rack plates. The process, or at least an adaptation of it, is still used today. In 1889 he recruited a modeller called Charles Noke, a man whose name is now synonymous with many of the best-loved Royal Doulton figures. He was responsible for many developments within the business and for modelling many new shapes. This talent was quickly recognised by John Slater and Noke became his assistant responsible for the work of the other artists.

The Burslem artists added the finishing touches to the various shapes and types of glazed bodies that came from the factory. The work of many of these artists, such as David Dewsberry, Sam Wilson, Henry Mitchell, Edward Raby, Louis Bilton, Joseph Hancock, Walter Slater, Harry Piper and George White, fetch premium prices at auctions these days. Samuel Wilson, known more widely as Sam, was an artist of great ability. He specialised in placid landscapes with

deer and cattle grazing whilst his studies of fish and game and hunting scenes are amongst the best ever painted on china. In 1894 Princess Louise commissioned Wilson to paint a dessert service as a gift from her to her mother Queen Victoria on the occasion of the Queen's Diamond Jubilee.

A contemporary of Wilson's was Henry Mitchell who also contributed to the success of the World's Columbian Exposition in Chicago in 1893. With Wilson, he painted the highly-acclaimed Diana vases that were a main feature of the Royal Doulton stand at the exhibition. Mitchell was a versatile artist and his skill can be seen on a wide variety of work from seashore themes of shells and seaweed to landscapes.

Louis Bilton brought a touch of the unusual and exotic to Royal Doulton china. Having trained at Minton under the former Sèvres artist William Mussill, Bilton travelled to Australia where he stayed for a number of years. On his return to Stoke-on-Trent and to the Royal Doulton factory, his sketchbooks of Australian flowers were quickly used as a source of inspiration for designs by him and other artists and decorators on a wide range of china vases and other ornamental shapes.

Father and son, Enoch and Harry Piper started work for the Company in 1892. Enoch specialised in heraldic designs and painted the crests of many British and foreign royal families as well as the nobility and regimental insignia. Harry Piper was an outstanding flower painter who made roses his speciality. His work was greatly sought after at the turn of the century, especially by American stores such as Tiffany in New York.

Many of the artists at Burslem tended to avoid figure painting and concentrated on fauna and flora, but George White made figure and portrait painting his own domain. White added the figures to the Diana vases that had also been decorated by Mitchell and Wilson and also painted portraits on china of Sir Henry Doulton as well as Henry's brother and partner James. I am lucky enough to have

Rembrandt Ware. A technique using coloured slips developed by Charles Noke and used for reproducing images from the Dutch 'Old Masters'.

Plate, with photograph of Kaiser Wilhelm II, grandson of Queen Victoria and Emperor of Germany 1888 to 1918. The photograph was reproduced by John Salter's patent process c1888.

Plate, Ducks painted by Samuel Wilson, 1902.

George White's magnificent portrait of Sir Henry, mounted in a deep brown velvet surround and framed in a dark leather case, at my home. The china background gives the face of the portrait a strange, almost life-like translucence and the shine from the glaze of the china surface makes the eyes of the portrait twinkle in the light.

The Chicago Exhibition of 1893 was the first large and prominent display of Burslem wares. It gave Sir Henry the showcase he desired to reveal the fine quality and artistry of his staff. The stand displayed the amazing variety of shapes and glazes that the Company could produce as well as the exemplary achievements of his artists. For this exhibition Sir Henry constructed twin arcaded pavilions, linked by a central domed hall, all built of the Company's ornate terracotta tiles. In the hall there was a coloured tile frieze showing the processes of pottery-making. A central attraction was George Tinworth's huge vase, over four feet tall, showing the 'History of England'.

The five-feet high Diana vase, the work of a number of the Doulton studio artists was topped by a figure of Diana the huntress with her hounds at her feet. This exhibition saw the first display of Royal Doulton figures, including Jack Point, Moorish Minstrel, Lady Jester and A Jester (seated), all the work of Noke.

The Exhibition was the jewel in Sir Henry's crown, it proved without doubt that the Burslem Potteries were not only innovative, but also that they were established and highly successful. The achievements of Royal Doulton at Burslem and Lambeth were summed up in the *Art Journal*

Review of that year. 'Seldom has it happened in the experience of a single generation to see the birth and complete development of an entirely new Art Industry,' it said. The *Review* continued 'Yet in the short space of some twenty years there has been originated and perfected at the Lambeth potteries, without the aid of previous tradition, a wealth of ceramic method that seems likely to become a conspicuous feature of that Renaissance of English Art which dated from the Victorian era.'

Sir Henry J. Wood, one of the Royal Commissioners for the exhibition and a member of the Council of the Society of Arts, also wrote great praises of the Company. He described the Royal Doulton stand as 'The finest collection of pottery I have ever known to be forwarded by an individual exhibitor to any international exposition. In saying that I do not except even the magnificent collection sent from Sèvres, the French government factory, but taken altogether this collection of Doulton's is the finest ever seen.' Sir Philip Cunliffe-Owen, Director of the South Kensington Museum added his praise, describing the exhibition 'Henry Doulton's greatest triumph.' But this praise did not go to Sir Henry's head or slow down the progress and development in the studios of Burslem.

Pieces made from bone china and painted in the Art Studios, Burslem. Left to right: Oval dish, Dendrobium Devonianum, painted by David Dewsberry, 1903; Pair of Vases, Lovers after Boucher painted by Leslie Johnson, c1915; Teapot, Exotic Birds, painted by J Birbeck, c1915.

In the following years more lines were introduced. Charles Noke created Holbein Ware, amongst other techniques, the glaze and paint effect that gives the appearance of an 'Old Master' painting. This finish was achieved by applying liquid clay onto a hard-fired porcelain body made from kaolin (china clay) and feldspar (an aluminium-based mineral). Rembrandt Ware was similar in appearance to Holbein, but with a heavy brown background and decorated with a portrait, quotes or text from an old master. Kingsware was also developed at this time, with

Dante vase, modelled by Charles Noke and painted by George White, exhibited at Chicago 1893.

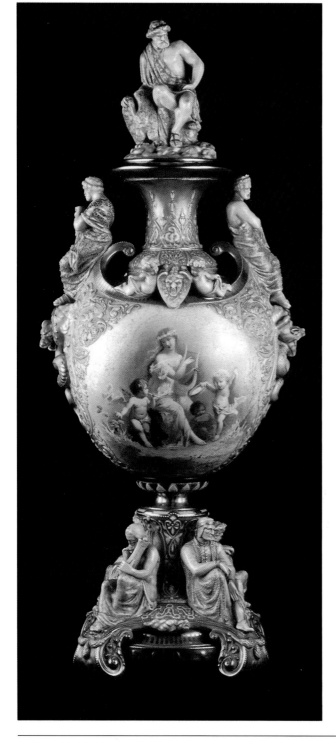

Vase painted with peonies by Edward Raby, c1896.

Centrepiece with modelled mermaids and shells by Charles Noke,
exquisite gilding of seaweed and octopus by William Hodkinson.
Exhibited at Chicago, 1893.

One of the seven gold awards presented to Doulton and Co at the Chicago Exhibition, 1893.

decoration formed in the mould, rather than painted on afterwards, by means of coloured slip. Noke was also responsible for the delicate Hyperion Ware, Luscian and Lactolian wares both in paler velvety finishes with hand-painted floral and woodland scenes. Lustreware was another of his discoveries and the metallic sheen that inspired the name was created by a glaze containing particles of metal.

The late 1890s saw a period of still further and greater advancement. Charles Noke and John Slater set about trials to create glazes and finishes inspired by those used by Chinese potters during the Sung Dynasty. By 1904 Slater, Noke, Bailey's son Cuthbert and a consultant Bernard Moore, had prepared the first few pieces of an exciting range called Flambé Ware. These few early pieces were launched at the St Louis Exhibition that year and Royal Doulton won a medal. This unique, dramatic black and red ware is still popular today.

Interest in things Chinese was heightened by the Boxer Rebellion and other uprisings that were taking place in China around this time. Many British colonial families fled from the East bringing home with them exciting and unusual ceramics that were rare or unseen in this country. By the time Flambé Ware, with its firey overtones and contrasting shading, was in production, the market for such ware was at its peak. The 1920s saw Chinoiserie at the height of fashion. Interiors were decorated in red and black, lacquered furniture and chintz and damask fabrics printed with oriental themes were all the rage.

Royal Doulton produced Flambé vases, bowls, sculpted figures and animals and even coffee services. From that time Flambé has remained a special but popular part of our work. In 1988 we launched the Images of Fire collection which shows the lustre and richness of this glaze to its best advantage on simple but stylishly modelled animal sculptures. Special edition figures for the Collectors Club and limited edition pieces have been issued.

There are only a few people who know the secret formula used to create Flambé. I was very honoured on one occasion

– yes, only once – to be allowed into the special department where the process takes place. Even then the ingredients were not divulged and some of my more probing questions were politely ignored or only answered vaguely.

There is a wonderful old tale said to date back to the ancient potters in China. The tale relates that there once was a potter who was trying to produce a glaze as green as jade, but each time he fired his pots they came out black. This went on for some time until one day he emptied the kiln and found that he had one magnificent red vase. The red vase was so beautiful and unusual that it was sent as a gift to the Emperor. The Emperor was so taken with the extraordinary vase that he ordered four more. The poor potter was distraught and, no matter how hard he tried to recreate the red glaze, the pots kept coming out black. Eventually, beside himself with anxiety, the potter threw himself into the kiln. His fellow potters tried in vain to save him, but it was too late. As they cooled and emptied the kiln the potter's friends discovered that all the vases were covered with a magnificent red glaze.

No such drastic measures are employed in our Flambé department, as the glaze is produced by means of a precise and controlled formula. The Flambé department is well hidden inside the large Nile Street buildings. Large sliding metal doors seal the kiln off from the main studio and visitors' area. Melvin, with his wry smile and starched white coat, is in charge of Flambé production and has worked in this hallowed department for more than thirty-five years. Arthur, has more than thirty years to his credit and Pat, a comparative newcomer, has served twenty years.

There is a sort of unofficial Official Secrets Act that binds the team, and with stop watches and memorised procedures they create the special rich glaze. Melvin, who says he can count the number of visitors to his department on the fingers of one hand, admits to being biased towards Flambé. He says he would add a Flambé glaze to any piece of china the Company produced, but then again he is a self-confessed addict of this technique. All the information that I gathered from my one visit to the Flambé department was that the glaze contains copper oxide which forms into a curious, velvety brown coating when fired in a carefully monitored kiln. This soft brown powder is carefully washed away and as it dissolves the vibrant red glaze appears from underneath – like magic.

I have a soft spot for Flambé Ware myself, and have a number of pieces at home. Personally I think it looks best on simple animal shapes and some of the figures, such as the Genie and the Geisha, that have an oriental theme.

In 1915, the Noke and Bailey team developed yet another new glaze called Titanian. The name came from the titanium oxide which gives the glaze its soft colouring, varying from cloudy grey through powder blue to a rich, royal blue. The glaze provided a background for detailed, hand-painted pictures.

The Chinese theme was enlarged with the addition of Sung Ware. These pieces had a backgound of Flambé glaze but were overpainted and gilded to achieve a truly elaborate effect. Underwater scenes with fishes, exotic birds and pixies in enchanted woods were all popular themes. The appearance of real Chinese jade was also imitated with glazes and used mostly on objects with an oriental feel. Yet another orientally-inspired range was Chang Ware, popular in the middle of the Roaring '20s and as richly decorated as Sung Ware. Chang Ware was made by applying several

Figures decorated with the rich Rouge Flambé glaze and introduced in 1990. Left to right: The Wizard (HN3121, Alan Maslankowski); Lamp Seller (HN3278, Robert Tabbenor); Carpet Seller (HN2776, Bill Harper); and Genie (HN2999, Robert Tabbenor).

Vases and dishes decorated with Rouge Flambé, Sung Titanian and Crystalline glazes, 1915 to c1950.

Samurai Warrior (HN3402, in Rouge Flambé glazes, Robert Tabbenor, introduced in 1992).

layers of thick glazes and allowing them to run over each other, like hot chocolate sauce on ice-cream. The mixing and blending of the colours created a spectrum of shades, but no two pieces could ever be made to match.

During the Second World War the manufacturing of Flambé Ware was almost stopped, but it was revived afterwards. Many of the more unusual glazes, although part of an important and experimental phase, quickly fell out of fashion and production ceased. But the strong tradition of experiment and development still exists within the Company to this day and glaze trials are just one of the many investigations carried out in the design department.

A piece of history and a reminder of the family past can be found at West Norwood cemetery in south London. It is the final resting place of Sir Henry Doulton, his father John and other people of interest and influence in the Doulton family and business. My father used to visit this cemetery once or twice a year and on one such occasion he took me with him. As a child the thought of visiting a graveyard filled me with dread, my imagination ran riot with thoughts of ghosts and spectres. When my father produced a large, iron key from his coat pocket, with the intention of opening the ornate iron gates which led to the interior of the terracotta Doulton mausoleum, I was on the point of hysteria. But after some gentle persuasion and spurred on by overwhelming curiosity, I finally stepped inside. Once through the gates I lost all trace of fear and marvelled at the ornate ceiling and the cool tranquillity of the soft buff and orange tiled tomb. The ceiling, covered in thousands of tiny pieces of mosaic in dark blue, light blue, burgundy red and tiny, glistening gold stars, shone in the sunlight that came through the Gothic arched, coloured glass windows.

Years later I returned to West Norwood cemetery with my wife Pruna, and although the key to the mausoleum had been mislaid we managed to look through the wrought iron gates into the sunset shades of the terracotta interior. The ceiling and sparkling stars were still in perfect condition. Outside there are several small figures of bishops with highly decorated mitres and angels with downturned wings. Above the gates and at the back of the tomb are two magnificent panels of angels and lambs. One can only guess that they may be the work of George Tinworth, who lies buried in the same plot as his mother, near the gates of the same cemetery.

The quality and detail of the work in this Doulton memorial is a just tribute to Sir Henry's enterprising and entrepreneurial spirit. His encouragement of the arts and foresight in business earned him a place amongst the most eminent men of his era.

The mausoleum is also the resting place of Sir Henry's wife of forty years, Sarah (née Kennaby) and their eldest son Henry Lewis Doulton who was Chairman of the Company until 1930. Six other members of the family, the last buried in 1932, are also commemorated. Further down the hill in the non-consecrated section of the cemetery, because the family were non-conformist rather than Church of England, there is another interesting group of family graves. Sir Henry's father John, his mother and several other members of the family are interred beneath a tall, pink granite monument. To the left, beneath a grey stone slab are John Watts and his family. Watts was John Doulton's partner in 1815 when the business was founded.

Just a little way behind these two tombs is another terracotta memorial. This is the resting place of James Baldwin Brown and his family. James had met John Doulton when they were at school and they formed a friendship that lasted throughout their lives. One can conjecture that the ornate terracotta monument might have come from John Doulton's Lambeth pottery.

This resting place of John, Sir Henry, family, friends and business colleagues is a fascinating place to visit. Many other grand Victorian gentlemen and women are buried here. Sir Henry Tate of the Tate & Lyle sugar company and founder of the Tate Gallery is also interred in an impressive terracotta mausoleum. The tiles of this Tate monument may well have been made by Doulton's Lambeth factory. A contemporary of Sir Henry's, Sir Henry Bessemer FRS, a prolific inventor and the man who founded the process for converting pig-iron into steel is also laid to rest in these grounds, as are Mrs Isabella Beeton, authoress of *Mrs Beeton's Book of Household Management* and Baron Paul Julius de Reuter, founder of the famous press agency. The work of the Friends of West Norwood Cemetery is much appreciated in the care and maintenance of this part of our family history.

THE SIR HENRY DOULTON SCHOOL OF SCULPTURE

During his lifetime Sir Henry encouraged sculptors and painters by establishing the Art Studio at Lambeth. When the Company moved to Stoke-on-Trent, the Art Director at that time, John Slater, also made it his business to assist local art school students in developing their talents at the Burslem and Nile Street studios. To this day Royal Doulton is active in promoting and developing artistic talent. In 1986 the Company founded and continues to sponsor, with others, the Sir Henry Doulton School of Sculpture in Stoke-on-Trent. The School is a charitable trust and a unique institution offering the only purely figurative sculpture course in the country. Since its doors opened the school has been inundated with applications from would-be students.

The work of a number of the successful sculpture students greets you as you arrive at the main gates to the School. A full-size figure of a man in pale grey, slate resin stands like a sentry by the blue railings. Behind him a striking piece called 'Under Sail', inspired by Njord, the Norwegian god of Boats, sweeps majestically across the lawns. The local tourist board were so impressed by the figures that they asked permission to include them in a list of sights to see when visiting the city. Principal Rosemary Barnett, herself a noted sculptor, feels that the public also appreciate this style of work. 'I believe the majority of the public prefer figurative sculpture because they can easily understand and appreciate the form,' she says. 'This style of sculpture has always been a central feature of European Art; think of all the great statues in Italy, France and England. The course we offer gives students an understanding of nature, history of art and the basic skills required to work with various materials,' she concludes.

From the hundreds of applications to attend the school, which cover young school-leavers to mature, established painters and school teachers, only seven will be successful. Funding for the school does limit the intake but the space required for the sculptors and their work is substantial. On a visit you may find a life-size horse rearing skywards, a full-size statue of a man and a number of life-size busts in progress. Easels of drawings, bags of clay, maquettes and smaller models from which the sculptors are working, line up around the studio walls.

The course takes two years to complete and during that time the students study anatomy, which involves visiting veterinary colleges and teaching hospitals. Life drawing and the history and philosophy of art, along with the technical skills of casting, carving, modelling and welding are all covered. In the second year of the course the students start working towards their final shows. In the past these shows have been a great success with students not only selling work but also receiving commissions. In 1988 the students exhibited at Keele University with Britain's foremost sculptor, the late Dame Elisabeth Frink, who opened the Sculpture School and was Patron; she also visited the students in Stoke and invited them to her own studios. The students' graduation work has also been shown at other venues such as Royal Doulton, Piccadilly, and the crypt of St Martin-in-the-Fields, both in London.

The work produced by the students has also gained awards. Angela Munslow was a first-year student at the school when she won the competition to create the 'Discovery' statue for EXPO '92 in Seville. To illustrate the subject 'Discovery', Angela combined the fine china and crystal of the Royal Doulton Company in a four-foot high, female figure. The discovery this sculpture portrays is two-fold – firstly of womanhood and secondly of the crystal which she holds in her cupped hands. Angela used her 15-year-old next door neighbour, Sarah Carr, as a model for the figure. She also incorporated the four elements of earth, wind, fire and water, which are vital for the production of china.

The figure is the largest ever produced in Royal Doulton's factory and caused a number of headaches for the staff. The figure was divided into twenty-four mould parts and took about fifty gallons of slip to cast. Special supports had to be devised to hold the weight of the model and two men were needed, instead of the usual one, to pour a continuous flow of liquid slip into the moulds. A 12-inch high version of 'Discovery' was also made for sale. This smaller version was produced at the Nile Street factory alongside the rest of the normal-size figures, made up of just four parts.

Another Sculpture School pupil, Harry Everington, has his Nordic inspired 'Under Sail' sculpture displayed on the school's lawn. 'Under Sail' won the premier award in a competition held by the Royal Society of British Sculptors in 1991.

'Discovery' by Angela Munslow, the largest figure produced at the Nile Street factory required about 50 gallons of slip and two skilled craftsmen to handle the moulds. It was produced for display at EXPO'92, Seville, Spain. The lower body of 'Discovery' is being attached to the base and lower legs.

The Sculpture School has also been warmly received and supported by local businesses, suppliers and residents. Transport has been provided, free of charge, to take students and their work to exhibitions. Resin has been donated by Delta Resin Ltd of Stockport and clay and other basic materials have also been given to the school. Recently the School opened its doors for local residents to attend evening classes. The Sculpture School students help to pass on their knowledge to the keen amateurs and the classes have proved so popular that they are now held twice a week instead of once. The students say that they have learnt from their teaching experiences and that having a different view has helped them in understanding their subject.

There is no commercial pressure on the Sculpture School students; the course is not vocational or linked to the modelling studios in the Royal Doulton Company. Only one graduate has joined the Company, Amanda Hughes-Lubeck, mentioned in Chapter 2 for her work with animal models at the Beswick studios. Other graduates have gone on to become successful independent sculptors, such as Mark Delf. Another, David Goode, models the famous and notorious for Madame Tussaud's famous waxworks in London. Other students go on to teach or pursue further education at the Royal College of Art or similar establishments.

The first principal at the Sculpture School, Colin Melbourne, modelled a stately bronze statue of Sir Henry Doulton for the 1986 National Garden Festival in Stoke-on-Trent. When the Festival closed the sculpture was moved to a new home in the centre of Burslem, near to the Royal Doulton factory. Buried beneath the statue is a time capsule which may be unearthed sometime in the future. The capsule contains six items which give a flavour of life in Stoke-on-Trent in the 1990s. The items, chosen by local resident Mrs Marjorie Whalley through a competition, are the Royal Doulton figure Top o'the Hill (HN1834); Arnold Bennett's novel *The Card*, a Royal Doulton Carlyle plate; Stoke-on-Trent City Guide; an oatcake (vacuum sealed); and a copy of the local newspaper, the *Evening Sentinel*. Who knows, when the time capsule is opened, Top o'the Hill may still be one of our best-selling figures!

Discovery (HN3428, Angela Munslow). Available only in 1992.

Illustration from the book presented to Henry Lewis Doulton (see p105) by Arthur E. Pearce.

A range of floral jewellery is produced. Illustrated here are horseshoe-shaped brooches formed by tiny hand-made and hand-painted ceramic flowers. The centre blooms are a daisy, a carnation, an orchid and a rose with added tiny forget-me-nots, buds and leaves.

Examples of the different shapes used for commemoratives. Left to right: Figure of Queen Anne (limited edition of 5,000, Pauline Parsons, 1988); Plate depicting Queen Victoria, to commemorate her Golden Jubilee, 1897; Loving Cup to celebrate the marriage of The Prince of Wales and Lady Diana Spencer, 1982; Character Jug, King Charles I, commemorating the 350th Anniversary of the English Civil War (Bill Harper, 1992).

Chapter 7
COMMEMORATIVES

ROYAL CONNECTIONS AND COMMEMORATIVE WARE

'Commemorative' is the name given to figures, plates, Character Jugs or vases among other shapes which are made to record a significant event or to honour a person. The very founding of the Company, by my great, great, great grandfather in the year of the Battle of Waterloo, proved auspicious because many such events and anniversaries have since been commemorated by Royal Doulton. In 1831 the whole Company went by boat from Lambeth to see the opening of the new London Bridge by King William IV, and this respect for Royalty has inspired our productions ever since. Today, commemoratives are a colourful and interesting part of our manufacture and include Royal events, famous persons and political anniversaries thus reflecting the history of the world.

Perhaps the most popular type of commemorative and the one for which we have established a special reputation is that with a 'Royal' subject. We have produced both elaborate and simple pieces to mark events such as marriages, christenings, coronations and to commemorate Royal visits to Royal Doulton.

In April 1984 Her Royal Highness The Princess of Wales carried on a Royal tradition that has become a much treasured part of Royal Doulton's proud history when she visited our factory in Nile Street, Burslem. Her Majesty Queen Elizabeth (as Princess Elizabeth) had visited the same site on a rainy day in 1949 as had Her Majesty Queen Elizabeth The Queen Mother, when she was Duchess of York, in 1931.

During the most recent Royal visit to our factory in Stoke-on-Trent the Princess of Wales toured part of the factory and met one of our long-serving flowermakers Ruth Ford. Ruth was putting the finishing touches to a miniature representation of the Princess's bridal bouquet to be added to the model of Her Royal Highness in her wedding dress (HN2887). The Princess was fascinated at the tiny scale of Ruth's work.

The Princess of Wales poured liquid clay slip into the mould of the Little Boy Blue (HN3035) figure. The Princess described the process to our Managing Director at that time, Sir Richard Bailey, as being similar to 'pouring gravy'. The Little Boy Blue figure that the Princess had cast, was subsequently fired, painted and finished and it was sent to her as a memento of her day at Royal Doulton.

The Princess was also asked to accept some pieces of

HRH The Princess of Wales casting an example of the figure 'Little Boy Blue' from the Nursery Rhymes Collection (HN3055) during her visit to Royal Doulton, 1985.

Bunnykins for the infant Prince William and the then Art Director responsible for Bunnykins tableware, Walter Hayward, was presented to Her Royal Highness. No doubt these have since been used by Prince William's younger brother Harry. We are honoured that Bunnykins has long been popular in Royal nurseries, for The Prince of Wales, The Princess Royal and their brothers all used it as children.

The tradition of Royal visits can be traced back to the time when The Prince of Wales (later Edward VII) presented Henry Doulton with the Albert Medal of the Society of Arts at the Lambeth factory in 1885. Queen Victoria did not actually visit the factory, but spent much time watching a potter throw a vase on a wheel, at the Doulton stand at the Liverpool Exhibition in 1885. One of Doulton's noted artists Arthur Pearce decorated the vase and it was later presented to

Queen Victoria, joining a collection of other pieces previously given to The Queen by Henry Doulton.

The first Royal visit to Burslem was in 1894. Princess Louise, the third daughter of Queen Victoria, and her husband the Marquis of Lorne visited the decorating and painting departments of the factory. The Princess saw the modelling of figures depicting the actor Henry Irving and the actress Ellen Terry, and in the showroom inspected the work of artists including Robert Allen, Samuel Wilson, George White and Louis Bilton.

In 1913 the Burslem Pottery had a second Royal day. The preparations for the visit involved erecting huge platforms for potters and men doing casting work. The potters and casters came from the factory and gave displays of their work to The King and Queen because it was now thought unseemly for Royalty to go inside such a place of work. But one tradition that has changed little in the sixty and more years between King George's and the Princess of Wales's visits, was the greeting given by the ladies of the factory. As King George V and Queen Mary came through the Nile Street gates, a line of young apprentices held up plates spelling out the greeting 'Your Majesty's Loyal Potters', an event which is immortalised in a black and white photograph hanging on the wall at the Sir Henry Doulton Gallery.

A similar style of welcome was offered to Princess Diana when she visited Nile Street in 1984. The ladies gave the Princess a less formal but no less meaningful plate-painted

Bunnykins pieces produced to commemorate the visit of HRH The Princess of Wales to Royal Doulton, 1985. Designed by Walter Hayward.

HRH The Princess Elizabeth (now The Queen) examining a range of commemorative beakers and mugs during her visit to Royal Doulton, 1949.

greeting, saying 'Welcome to Our Princess'. This time our thoroughly modern Princess toured the factory, and no special display stands were erected in the courtyard for her visit.

In 1949, Queen Elizabeth II, whilst Princess Elizabeth, visited the Nile Street factory in Burslem at the end of the Second World War. Her Majesty was escorted through the showrooms by Charles Noke and her equestrian tastes led her immediately to a display of horse models. To her surprise and pleasure The Princess was presented with a model of her own steeplechaser Monaveen which the modeller W.M. Chance had secretly created with the help of the horse's trainer. It took twenty-six separate moulds and five firings to complete the piece. My father met the then Princess Elizabeth, at the presentation of Monaveen and was impressed by her knowledge of the Company and the manufacturing processes involved in making the horse model. The only other example of Monaveen is in the Sir Henry Doulton Gallery at the Nile Street factory.

Events associated with the Prince and Princess of Wales have always been popular. The Princess of Wales was the subject of two figures by Royal Doulton to commemorate her wedding on 29 July 1981. Her marriage also inspired the additions to the historic range of commemorative wares. A special beaker, limited edition plate and limited edition loving cup were produced to mark the event. The loving cup and plate were designed by Neil Faulkner and a portrait of the Royal couple formed the centrepiece of both items. The plate was bordered with fine gold tracery and delicately coloured sprays of English oak, daffodils in honour of The Prince of Wales and English roses in honour of Lady Diana Spencer.

His Royal Highness, The Prince of Wales has also been depicted as a Royal Doulton figure. To complete the wedding duo, the Prince was modelled in his dashing uniform as Colonel-in-Chief of the Welsh Guards (HN2884) and another figure (HN2883) shows Prince Charles in the ermine and purple velvet robes he wore at his Investiture as Prince of Wales. For this event in 1969, Royal Doulton produced a limited edition of 150 black basalt busts of The Prince, modelled by John Bromley. In 1972 similar style busts were made of The Queen and Duke of Edinburgh to celebrate their silver wedding anniversary.

One of Prince Charles's most unusual pieces of Royal Doulton must be an 1895 Doulton Water Closet. Like his distinguished father, Prince Charles has been known to mix official pronouncements with light-hearted asides, some of which make their way into newspaper columns. During a speech The Prince commented that he was fascinated by old lavatories. Antique dealer James Cunningham and London club owner Peter Rosengard took the comment as a Royal Command and took it upon themselves to track down the highly ornate 1895 Doulton Water Closet. The pair of loyal subjects duly delivered their china gift to Buckingham Palace, but it is not known whether The Prince has had it installed at Buckingham Palace, at Kensington Palace or his country home Highgrove, or whether it is, in fact, in use!

In the same year as the Royal Wedding, Prince Philip celebrated his sixtieth birthday. This event was marked by Royal Doulton with a figure of Prince Philip (HN2386). The Prince is portrayed in the full dress uniform of an Admiral of the Fleet. Modeller Peggy Davies reproduced the uniform in minute detail down to the insignia and decoration of his grand attire.

The birth of The Prince and Princess of Wales's first child, Prince William, was commemorated with a two-handled Bunnykins mug and a book-shaped savings bank both inscribed 'To Celebrate the Birth of the First Child of TRH The Prince and Princess of Wales, 1982'. A limited edition eight-inch plate was also produced to commemorate the event. The design for the plate featured two cherubs entwined with garlands forming a ring around a scroll which bears the inscription. The plate is further decorated with flowers, doves and blue ribbons in honour of the little Prince and was designed by Neil Faulkner.

Collectors of commemoratives concentrate on different aspects, some enthusiasts attempt to collect everything whilst others limit their interest. Collector John Shaw started his now sizeable collection of Royal commemorative ware as a boy. He remembers watching Queen Elizabeth's Coronation on a crackly black and white television. The excitement of the event triggered his interest in memorabilia, which he latterly narrowed down to collecting Royal Doulton ware from Queen Victoria's Golden Jubilee up to Queen Elizabeth II's Coronation.

Coronations and their anniversaries is one theme that would provide a varied collection, and one that would reflect a wealth of historical interest. Royal Doulton have a long and highly-regarded record in making this kind of china. The variety of creative shapes which have been used as royal commemoratives give an insight into the international history of collecting within this theme.

Such a collection could range from the most recent, the fortieth anniversary of the Coronation of Queen Elizabeth II in 1993, to the Coronation of Queen Victoria in 1837, and can include all the monarchs who have reigned in between. There is a vast choice of shapes – beakers, mugs, plates, vases and figures – from which to choose, and pieces were made at both the Burslem and Lambeth factories.

The first Royal commemorative wares produced at the Burslem factory arose through the friendship of The Prince of Wales (later King Edward VII) and Sir Henry Doulton. In 1887, the Prince arranged a great party for children in Hyde Park to mark the Golden Jubilee of the Coronation of his mother, Queen Victoria. Sir Henry Doulton, 'By Appointment Potter to HRH The Prince of Wales', was asked to suggest some ideas for a souvenir which could be given to the children. Several ideas were suggested but The Prince did not approve of them. However, during a visit to Russia The Prince saw a commemorative beaker he liked, and on a piece of paper, he made a rough sketch of the shape. On his return home, the Prince handed the sketch to Sir Henry, saying that it was this simple shape that he wanted. Working on this idea John Slater designed the decoration and the project was finally given the go-ahead by The Prince. The Company produced over 100,000 earthenware beakers of this style decorated with a single colour brown transfer print showing the head of the young and old Victoria. Although a large number were produced, few have survived the rigours of time and so the price for such an item is rising.

Ten years later, to celebrate Queen Victoria's Diamond Jubilee, the Burslem pottery fulfilled a commission to celebrate the 'record reign'. Three designs of beakers in five different colourways were made. The beakers could also be enamelled in a variety of colours and supplied with a gold edge or a completely gold finish. Local councils and other societies throughout Britain also commissioned quantities of the beakers with special inscriptions for presentation purposes.

A catalogue page illustrating commemoratives produced at the Lambeth factory to celebrate the Coronation of George V and Queen Mary and the Investiture of The Prince of Wales.

ROYAL DOULTON POTTERIES.

"Coronation Doultonware"

x 7456 "Coronation" Set.

Doultonware Relief Decorations.

Loving Cup (1-qt.) **3/9**   Jug (1-qt.) **3/9**   Tobacco Jar (½-lb.) **3/6**

Mug (¾-pint) to match **2/-**

TO mark the auspicious occasion of the Coronation of Their Majesties King George V. & Queen Mary (whom may God preserve), Messrs. Doulton & Co. introduce these designs in their Lambeth Stoneware. Each piece bears portrait medallions of their Majesties and appropriate emblems.

x7455 "Coronation" Set, Doultonware; Heraldic Colourings with Gilding.

Jug (1-qt.) **4/-**	Tobacco Jar (½-lb.) **4/-**	Teapot (1½-pts.) **3/9**	Mug (¾-pt.) **2/9**	Loving Cup (1-qt.) **4/9**
x 7455 a THE SAME DESIGNS BUT PLAIN PRINTED ONLY.				
. . . **2/-**	. . . . . . **2/-**	. . . . . **1/9**	. . . . **1/3**	. . . . **2/6**

In harmony with the last, a similarly decorated set is issued in commemoration of the **INVESTITURE AT CARNARVON CASTLE OF H. R. H. THE PRINCE OF WALES.**

x 7457 "Investiture" Set, Doultonware; Heraldic Colourings with Gilding.

Loving Cup (3-pts.) **4/-**	Tobacco Jar (½-lb.) **3/-**	Mug (¾-pt.) **2/-**	Jug (1-qt.) **3/9**
x 7457 a THE SAME DESIGNS BUT PLAIN PRINTED ONLY.			
. . . . . . **2/3**	. . . . . . **1/6**	. . . . **1/3**	. . . **1/9**

DOULTON & Co., Limited., LAMBETH, LONDON, S.E.

By Appointment Potters to H.M. King George V.

Commemoratives to mark the 40th anniversary of The Queen's accession to the throne in 1992 and Coronation in 1993. Left to right: The Queen (HN3440, Peter Gee, 1992, limited edition of 3,500); Plate designed by Neil Faulkner, limited edition of 2,500; Queen Elizabeth II (HN3436, Alan Maslankowski, 1993, limited edition of 5,000), available through Lawleys-by-Post.

In 1901 'Victoria in memoriam' beakers were produced. They marked not only Queen Victoria's death but the end of the Victorian era. These beakers were decorated with a portrait of The Queen wearing a blue sash against the background of a purple heart. On the back the inscription read 'Died at Osborne, Jany 22nd 1901'. Few of these beakers were produced and they are very rare. Some, with commas instead of full stops in the inscription, are even more unusual.

When The Queen's son was crowned King Edward VII the Company were again summoned to produce a special piece to commemorate the event. From *The Daily Telegraph's* Court Circular of 24 March 1902 comes the announcement, 'Mr. R.D. Doulton had the honour of being received by The King and submitting to His Majesty a specimen of the cups which are being made to commemorate The King's dinner on the occasion of His Majesty's Coronation'. Also made to commemorate the event were a pair of silicon busts of The King and his

Queen, Alexandra. These busts were modelled by a recent addition to Royal Doulton's design team, Leslie Harradine. Harradine was destined to become one of the most prolific and successful modellers of his time. Harradine made a similar set of busts in 1911 when King Edward was succeeded by his son George.

Elaborate relief modelled loving cups were produced in the 1930s to celebrate the Coronations and anniversaries of that period. In 1952 HM Queen Elizabeth II ascended to the throne and in 1953 one of these intricate loving cups designed by Jack Noke marked the event.

In 1973 a figure of Queen Elizabeth II was modelled by Peggy Davies (HN2502) and released in a limited edition of 750 to celebrate the twentieth anniversary of The Queen's Coronation in 1953. Ten years later another figure of HM Queen Elizabeth (HN2878) appeared dressed in state robes of royal blue and red, with gold tassels, honours and decorations. This later model, by Eric Griffiths, was released in a limited edition of 2500 to mark the thirtieth anniversary of Her Majesty's Coronation. The figure, at ten and a half inches, is bigger than the normal HN figures of between seven and eight inches.

Both the fortieth anniversary of The Queen's accession to the throne and her Coronation have been commemorated by the Company. Two beautifully detailed figures have been modelled by Alan Maslankowski and Peter Gee. These are both in limited editions. Other pieces have also been produced for these anniversaries, one is a plate designed by Neil Faulkner with a border of national emblems inspired by colours of a chair in Westminster Abbey. The second is a loving cup, the first made by Royal Doulton for over ten years and this is in a limited edition of 2500.

One popular and well-loved member of the Royal Family cannot be overlooked in this brief introduction to Royal commemoratives. HM Queen Elizabeth The Queen Mother has inspired our modellers who have portrayed her warm and friendly nature in figure models and on other shapes. A limited edition of 1500 models was made to commemorate the eightieth birthday of HM Queen Elizabeth The Queen Mother on 4 August 1980. The figure was made to match the earlier figure of Queen Elizabeth II issued in 1973; and

Five of the many beakers issued since 1897 to commemorate Royal events. Left to right, top row: Beaker to celebrate the marriage of Princess May with Viscount Lascelles, 28th February 1922; Beaker to commemorate the Coronation of Edward VII and Queen Alexandra, 1902. Bottom row: Beaker in memory of Queen Victoria, 1901; Beaker given at the 'Coronation Dinner' held by King Edward VII to celebrate his Coronation, 1902; Beaker to commemorate the Coronation of King George V and Queen Mary, 1911.

Above: A contemporary illustration showing the Jubilee beaker given to children at a party in Hyde Park organised by the then Prince of Wales, 1887.

Plate designed by Neil Faulkner to commemorate the 90th birthday of Queen Elizabeth The Queen Mother, limited edition of 1,000. Artwork is being placed into position to form the design for the completed plate, 1990. Courtesy of Peter Brooker, Rex Features Ltd.

she wears a full length pink and white gown, tiara, jewelled bracelet and the sash and star of The Order of the Garter. A commemorative loving cup and plate were also issued.

In 1990 a stunning new model of The Queen Mother (HN3189) was produced to mark the ninetieth birthday of this amazing lady. This model shows Her Majesty in a gown of pinks and blues with a fur wrap, and the sash of the Order of the Garter and holding a tiny posy of individually-created, yellow roses. A plate was also produced to celebrate her birthday and included designs by Neil Faulkner. A charming study of The Queen Mother as Duchess of York (HN3230) was created by Pauline Parsons. A loving cup and other commemorative ware was produced in 1937 when her husband The Duke of York became King, replacing his brother Edward who abdicated in order to marry 'the woman I love', Wallis Simpson.

Other pieces produced by the Company have Royal associations but have not been produced for a specific occasion. Monarchs from the past such as Queen Elizabeth I (HN3099), Queen Victoria (HN3125), Queen Anne (HN3141), King Charles (HN404), (HN2084) and (HN3459), Henry VIII (HN370, HN673, HN1792) and his wives have all been the subjects of Royal Doulton figure models.

The Queen Victoria figure, from The Queens of the Realm series modelled by Pauline Parsons was a limited edition introduced in 1987. Queen Victoria, Britain's longest reigning monarch, Empress of India and the ruler of the greatest Empire, is portrayed as a young woman. The model shows The Queen with her hair styled in a centre parting

King Edward VII (Bill Harper, introduced in 1992, limited edition 2,500, for the Royal Doulton International Collectors Club).

with a bun, as was fashionable at that time. She wears a soft pink dress trimmed with layers of lace-edged frills. The scoop neckline of her dress is enhanced by a small red rose-bud, perhaps alluding to the traditional symbol of the red rose of England. The Queen is portrayed with two of her

beloved King Charles spaniels, one standing on a stool, rising to the caress of her outstretched hand. The other brown and white spaniel is lovingly tucked under her other arm. Collecting Royal figures is a popular theme with a number of enthusiasts. The dazzling array of pieces with Royal associations also includes Character Jugs and King Charles I, Henry VIII and his wives, and most recently King Edward VII have also featured in this medium.

Royal Doulton is privileged to be commissioned by the Royal family to produce special pieces for their personal use. Knowledge of many of these special orders is restricted to provide privacy, however I am able to tell you of some that we have received. King Edward VII, who first granted the Company the Royal Warrant, commissioned a special dessert service hand-painted with baskets of flowers. This was carried out by Charles Brough and Percy Curnock. We were granted permission to retain several pieces for our museum collection. Queen Mary similarly commissioned many pieces. One table service was decorated with an intricate gold design on a pale apple green ground. Subsequently she permitted the design to be made available to the general public. Queen Mary also had a very special miniature tea service made for her famous doll's house which is now on public display at Windsor Castle. Each piece was modelled by Alfred Baker, and is hand-decorated and monogrammed with her insignia and bears the backstamp of Royal Doulton. A few pieces of this, the smallest of Royal Doulton tableware, can be seen at the Sir Henry Doulton Gallery.

In 1981 HRH The Prince of Wales commissioned Royal Doulton to make a limited edition range of plates. These plates are given away by The Prince, to various auctions and events for fund raising. The plate is decorated in sea green and gold, with three feathers, a crown and a furled ribbon

Two Royal commissions. Left, a cup and saucer produced for Queen Mary and subsequently available for general sale c1915. Right, a reproduction of a plate from a dessert service commissioned by Edward VII and originally painted by Charles Brough in 1905. This copy is by Percy Curnock.

Plate commissioned by HRH The Prince of Wales and designed by Lord Snowdon with Carl Toms, 1981.

with The Prince's motto 'Ich Dien' which is the German for 'I serve' as the central design. Based on The Prince of Wales's heraldic badge which dates back to the Black Prince of the fourteenth century, a border of laurel leaves completes the decoration. This design was by Carl Toms with Lord Snowdon. The badge of three feathers and motto are used only by the heir apparent and the special plates are, quite rightly, valued by their eventual purchasers.

A fascinating type of commemorative records exploration and discovery of new countries. Most recently the 500th anniversary of Christopher Columbus's discovery of the New World has been celebrated by the modelling of a figure by Alan Maslankowski and a Character Jug by Stanley Taylor. Both pieces are superbly decorated and have fine expressive detail. A small sized Character Jug was only available to members of the International Collectors Club.

Various commemoratives to mark anniversaries of the founding of countries have been produced. These include the 200th anniversary of the United States in 1976, when the Soldiers of the Revolution, with a different soldier representing each of the regiments of the original thirteen states were issued. These, in a limited edition of 350, are now highly collectable. The sailing of the Pilgrim Fathers from Plymouth on the *Mayflower* in 1620 was marked by a black basalt loving cup in 1970. The Canadian centennial was celebrated in 1967 with a series of three plates depicting Old Quebec; the Peace Tower and Houses of Parliament, Ottawa; and a map of Canada.

In 1988 the Australian Bicentennial range was made to commemorate the landing of Captain Arthur Phillip at

Botany Bay. In January 1788, after eight months at sea, the First Fleet of eleven ships and over 1000 people arrived on the South East Coast of Australia. The occupants of the ships were mostly convicts, transported to form the workforce of a British settlement governed by Captain Phillip. Royal Doulton's commemorative ware 200 years later included a limited edition loving cup showing the fleet at Port Jackson on one side, while on the other, images representative of Australia today, such as the Sydney Harbour Bridge and the famous Opera House, were featured. A special Bunnykins figure showed a bunny character waving the centennial flag and an impressive commemorative plate with the names of the eleven original ships and their masters around the rim was also created. In addition, an orange colourway of the figure Top o'the Hill was created to mark the event.

Also commemorating Australia's Bicentenary was the Royal Doulton black basalt figure of a Lyrebird with an upswept tail of acid-etched crystal, resting on a base of Tasmanian blackwood. This magnificent two and a half feet tall creation was the work of Jo Ledger, the Company's Design Director at the time. The Lyrebird was presented to the Museum of Victoria for the State Collection on the occasion of the visit of HM The Queen.

The anniversary of Captain Cook's discovery in 1770 of Australia was also marked. In 1933 a loving cup designed by Charles Noke and Harry Fenton was made to commemorate Captain Cook's landing at Botany Bay. In a limited edition of 350 the loving cup depicts a party of

Napoleon (HN3429, limited edition of 1,500, Alan Maslankowski, 1992).

Duke of Wellington (HN3432, limited edition of 1,500, Alan Maslankowski, 1992).

crewmen stepping ashore from a long-boat on one side and on the other side Cook is shown surveying the interior with a group of officers. The handles are in the shape of coconut palms with the Union Jack and Australian flags entwined around them. In 1970 another loving cup was produced to celebrate the 200th anniversary of Cook's landing. This dramatic black basalt cup depicts a group of Aborigines greeting the Captain and his crew as they row ashore from their ship *Endeavour*. On the reverse is a fine profile portrait of Captain Cook. The spirit of Cook's *Endeavour* lives on in the tall ship *Young Endeavour* which was the United Kingdom's Bicentenary gift in 1988 to the people of Australia. On board is specially-designed Royal Doulton tableware featuring the Southern Cross motif.

When New Zealand attained dominion status in 1907 Royal Doulton produced a special tableware pattern inspired by Maori art. The design, executed in vivid orange and black was originally offered on fine white china, but an earthenware version was introduced in 1928. The same Maori pattern was also used as a border on a series of Rack plates featuring New Zealand imagery. In the 1930s when it was announced that New Zealand would have independent status, a number of Royal Doulton pieces were produced including a now very rare 'Moko' Maori Character Jug. Moko is the traditional decorative scarring that the Maoris tattooed onto their faces and bodies.

Military history has frequently inspired our designers. Every campaign since the Crimean War has been commemorated by Royal Doulton. In recent times the Falklands War and the Gulf War were marked by two tankards under the title Return of the Canberra and Desert Storm. In 1990, to commemorate the fiftieth anniversary of the Battle of Britain, a limited edition of 14,750 tankards were produced. The illustration, by leading aviation artist

Commemoratives with an international theme. Left to right: Tankard, The Gulf War (designed by Geoff Hunt, limited edition of 14,750, 1991); Bunnykins figure (Warren Platt, specially produced to commemorate the Australian Bicentenary, 1988); Major, 3rd New Jersey Regiment, 1776 (HN2752, Eric Griffiths, from the Soldiers of the Revolution series, limited edition of 350, 1975); Loving Cup to commemorate the Australian Bicentenary, limited edition of 350.

Geoff Hunt, depicted Spitfires performing a victory roll with Hurricanes accompanying them in formation.

The military leaders Wellington, Nelson and Napoleon have been portrayed in many ways by the Company. My ancestor John Doulton was fascinated by their careers and in 1806 he spent his only day's holiday for the year attending the funeral service for Nelson held at St Paul's Cathedral, London! Between 1821 and 1830 figures, flasks and mugs were produced at Lambeth from saltglazed stoneware depicting these commanders. The centenary of the Battle of Trafalgar in 1905 inspired another collection of Lambeth pieces but this time many were decorated in the colourful glazes which we had developed by this time.

However it is the recent figures of Wellington, Nelson and Napoleon which have captured my imagination and I am sure would have delighted my great, great, great grandfather. These figures are all limited editions and were all modelled by Alan Maslankowski. The bases are decorated with scenes from the battles in which they fought, thus around the base of Nelson are illustrations from the Battle of Trafalgar. Also included are the flags which were used to carry messages to other ships in the fleet, bearing the message 'England expects that every man will do his duty'. Nelson is modelled holding his telescope, standing on the deck of his ship, *Victory*, while Napoleon and Wellington

are enhanced with metal accoutrements. All these figures required extensive research by Alan to ensure that all costumes and details were presented accurately. You can be sure that any slight mistake is noticed by someone who will very quickly let us know of the error. Nelson has also provided a fitting subject for the 1993 Character Jug of the Year. He is shown in full naval uniform with his ship *Victory* forming the handle. The modeller was the talented Stanley Taylor.

The theme of people and personalities can be extended as both older and modern statesmen such as Winston Churchill, George Washington, Abraham Lincoln, Sir John A. MacDonald, Ronald Reagan and Margaret Thatcher feature in a variety of formats. Character Jugs, figures, plates and loving cups have all been made. Literary names such as Dickens, Shakespeare, Tennyson and Longfellow and entertainers from Clark Gable and W.C. Fields to Laurence Olivier and Charlie Chaplin have all had their faces immortalised in clay and glaze.

As this is not a specialist book on commemorative wares I have mentioned only a small, but I hope tempting, sample of the products Royal Doulton has produced. There are

hundreds of different shapes and subjects to choose from with something to interest everyone, and collections can be as small or as extensive as you wish. New pieces are frequently introduced and many older pieces can be easily found. The more pricey early items can be difficult to locate but they give so much satisfaction when finally tracked down. There is no other Company quite like Royal Doulton for offering the choice and quality to commemorative collectors. If there is something worth commemorating Royal Doulton probably have a suitable piece of china available.

Political and historical characters have been commemorated in various ways by Royal Doulton. Left to right: The Statesman (HN2859, Bill Harper, 1988-1990). This model is a typical portrayal of a nineteenth century statesman. Loving Cup depicting Margaret Thatcher, to commemorate the election of the first female Prime Minister of the United Kingdom; Winston Churchill (HN3433, Alan Maslankowski, 1993, limited edition of 5,000); Character Jug of John Shorter (Bill Harper, 1990). The Shorter family has historical connections with Royal Doulton dating back to 1892 when John's grandfather became Royal Doulton's Australian agent; Character Jug of Abraham Lincoln (Stanley Taylor, 1992), President of the Union during the American Civil War, limited edition of 2,500.

Right: A group of Royal
Doulton red figures, a
popular colour with
collectors.
Left to right: Winsome
(HN2220, Peggy Davies,
1960-1986); Innocence
(HN2842, Eric Griffiths,
1979-1983); Christmas
Morn (HN1992, Peggy
Davies, introduced in
1947); Buttercup (HN2399,
Peggy Davies, introduced
in 1983); Lydia (HN1908,
Leslie Harradine,
introduced in 1939); and
Goody Two Shoes
(HN2037, Leslie Harradine,
1949-1989).

One of the unique aspects of Royal Doulton is the immense variety of its products, both today and in the past. Illustrated here are just
some of the pieces which are available to collectors.

Chapter 8
CARING FOR YOUR COLLECTION

Although collecting contemporary Royal Doulton china is extremely popular, there are also dedicated groups of collectors who seek out early examples of the Company's work. Some of these antique pieces are gaining in value and are auctioned by such notable houses as Phillips and Christie's. Mr Mark Oliver, the Royal Doulton specialist at Phillips, has accompanied me on a number of tours and has talked to members of the Collectors Club about our wares. Mark sums up Royal Doulton's present position as being well established in the modern market. 'Where Royal Doulton succeeds,' he observes, 'is in keeping the ball rolling for contemporary collectors. The Royal Doulton name is now synonymous with collecting.'

It is only comparatively recently that Royal Doulton has attained the recognition it was due. 'In the last fifteen years Royal Doulton has become widely recognised,' says Mark. A Royal Doulton enthusiast, Richard Dennis, put together a number of exhibitions in the early and mid-70s and these shows brought Royal Doulton to a larger public audience. Much early Doulton was undervalued; for example Victorian wares such as Slater's Patent and Silicon wares had a strange rather funereal appearance which was fashionable at that time. Amongst these pieces you see marvellous flashes of Victorian humour and the grotesque. These strange, Gothic-inspired styles are subject to the vagaries of fashion and prices can rise and fall depending on the vogue at the time. Mark points out, 'Some of the artwares produced by the artists in the Lambeth and Burslem studios are magnificent, they are individually-painted works of art. Valuations can be difficult; especially of the more unusual pieces. I have to imagine who would want the item, say an oddity such as a stoneware sundial made in the Lambeth factory. I have to evaluate how much I think someone would be willing to pay and how popular it might be at auction.'

Collectors are also keen on limited editions and discontinued pieces. Discontinued lines can be very recent,' says Mark, 'for example a Figure of the Year can increase in value in the following year, because it is no longer in production.' As soon as a figure or Character Jug is withdrawn from production its value starts to rise. You can also buy second-hand figures at auction and they may be sold for less than the shop value. These items are second-hand, do not come 'gift wrapped' and often have neither their boxes or certificates. Prices also vary according to the number of figures produced or the number still in

We welcome visitors to Royal Doulton factories. For information on factory tours, please see p. 141.

We welcome visitors to Royal Doulton factories. For information on factory tours, please see p. 141.

circulation. For example Top o'the Hill has been made since 1937, there may only be forty figures from the first year still on the market and these will command the greatest prices, whereas there are probably 400 or more from the 1980s so they will not fetch as much. A Royal Doulton collection can also be a worthwhile investment. 'In November 1991, Phillips' branch in New York sold a private collection of figures,' says Mr Oliver. 'There were over 1000 pieces in the collection accumulated over thirty years. Ninety-seven per cent of the lot was sold and that was during a time of financial recession.' That sort of sale is a good indicator of how Royal Doulton is keenly sought-after.

Mark Oliver has handled many rare and unusual pieces of old Doulton, including a unique George Tinworth clock which sold for £1800. He says, 'In the past the Company

produced the greatest diversity of products of any pottery manufacturer I know. Royal Doulton would turn their hands to anything, but they are also strong in specific areas such as figures and jugs. The interest to the collector is the choice of subjects to collect.' Indeed, there is something to appeal to almost everyone within the Royal Doulton ranges. From the Victorian richness and grandeur of the sophisticated, top-of-the-market, art-inspired goods by named artists, to the more sentimental and naive imagery of nurserywares, or the simple elegance of the Pretty Lady ranges.

Throughout this book I have given a brief outline of the development of Royal Doulton and its wares which, I hope, may help put the older styles of pottery, glazes and designs into some perspective and time-scale. One of the enduring features about Royal Doulton is the quality of the goods we make; the products created today are as good – if not better through advancements in technology – as those made when the Company started over 175 years ago. I have not gone into the detailed histories or full manufacturing processes for each range, but have given a brief explanation and description to aid recognition. For the avid collector who thirsts for further knowledge there are many excellent, specialist books on the various types of ware (some listed in the bibliography on page 142) which cover in depth both the historical and technical aspects.

RARE AND UNUSUAL ITEMS

Unusual items come to the surface in the Collectors Club magazine news section or through dealers and auction

houses. Prototypes are a real find. These are pieces that have never gone into production, items that have been withdrawn because they were thought to be uncommercial or too like another item in the range. Some of these pieces are brought up to the final stages, ie painted and glazed but often not backstamped or catalogued. Only a few of these items ever leave the factory, and usually not officially! They are in effect the only one of that particular design and therefore valuable for their rarity.

There have been a few cases of items being withdrawn after a brief production run, or in rare cases where there has been an inaccuracy in their design. The Character Jug of Anne Boleyn (D6644) caused us some embarrassment. The handle of the jug was modelled to portray an axe, but in fact Anne was executed in 1536 by a French swordsman who was specially brought to London from Calais.

Another example of a rare Character Jug is also one of Henry VIII's wives. The early production run of the Anne of Cleves Character Jug had a handle depicting a grey horse – because King Henry is said to have referred to her in a derogatory way as the 'Flanders mare'. The horse on the first batches of Character Jugs had erect ears but these proved difficult to manufacture and were often chipped or broken. This design was withdrawn and a revised model issued with the horse's ears flat to the side of its head

Character Jugs modelled in the Celebrity collection, but never put into general production. Left to right: Elvis Presley and Clark Gable, both by Stanley Taylor, and Marilyn Monroe and Humphrey Bogart, both by Eric Griffiths.

Two Character Jugs: Anne Boleyn (Douglas Tootle, 1975-1990); and The Red Queen (Bill Harper, 1987-1991).

DISPLAYING A ROYAL DOULTON COLLECTION

Whether you have one or one hundred pieces of Royal Doulton the care and attractive display of the china will ensure your continued enjoyment of your collection. For advice on caring for figures and other decorative items I have outlined some important points, but if you have any doubts it is always best to consult an expert.

For ideas on displaying your collection I have recalled examples and tips shown to me by shop display managers and in collectors' homes. Many imaginative ideas appear on the pages of home interest magazines and the numerous, well-illustrated books on house style. I must admit that we do not have any formal arrangement for our collection of Royal Doulton at home. I have all my Michael Doulton special figures, except two missing years, arranged on a couple of shelves. Our collection is really diverse, covering animals, Flambé Ware, figures of all sizes and Character Jugs, so we have opted for displaying them informally around our house instead of all in one room. The same is true of my mother's home. Her large collection, which covers historical and antique pieces as well as more recent pieces (she insisted that I give her the Character Jug of myself), is scattered throughout her house. From the hallway to the bedrooms and from the kitchen to the living room there is a mix of old and new together.

If you do have a special theme or type of collection there are many interesting ways of grouping and showing them. Some collectors have small groups of their treasures throughout their homes, others keep them all together in one place. I have been to homes in America where special extensions have been built to house a collection. In Britain the most common place for display is on the mantlepiece in a sitting or dining room and many careful collectors keep their Royal Doulton figures and Character Jugs behind the protective glass doors of a cabinet.

The method of display is a personal choice, but Royal Doulton collectors have, through the Collectors Club, revealed unusual and interesting ways of showing their collections. One artist/collector creates scenic views to act as a backdrop to his collection of Pretty Ladies. Talented painter Frank Daniell has made a mural landscape of Bunker Hill to provide a setting for his Soldiers of the Revolution group and, for his Royal Figures Collection, he has painted a background setting of the tree-lined entrance to Windsor Castle. Another collector has made a figure-sized doll's house complete with curtains, wallpaper and all the trimmings. In the house she keeps and displays her collection of Pretty Ladies. Each room holds a group of figures, looking as though they were in conversation or going about their daily chores. An American collector has divided each of the five main glass shelves of her display area into six sections. Each section is boxed on either side by a small partition, and within each 'kennel' box she shows a different breed of china Champion Dog.

Display blocks can help in achieving an attractive display. Rather than lining-up your figures in a regimental style, varying the height can be effective. The blocks can be used to lift items at the back of a shelf or mantlepiece, so that they can be viewed clearly above those in the foreground. Blocks can also be arranged to form a variety of shapes. A pyramid formation, for example, has the tallest block in the centre gradually sloping down by means of shorter blocks to the right and left. Placing objects on this graduated arrangement makes an eye-catching variation and can be used for Character Jugs, cups and saucers or where space is at a premium. Display blocks can be made of many materials. Small blocks of wood of varying heights, velvet-covered tin boxes, mirrors, glass, natural polished wood, cork or perspex are all possibilities. If you like plain wood you could stain and varnish or polish the surfaces to bring them up to a nice shine. You can decorate the blocks to complement the decoration of the room in which they will be placed.

Gilded and carved decorative wall brackets arranged in a triangular shape can transform a plain wall into a small gallery. The wider brackets have ample space to support a figure or can be used to display a collection of cups and saucers. Collectors of plates can try clear perspex or oriental-style polished wood stands for arrangements on window sills, shelves or mantlepieces. The stands hold the plates upright and are quite secure.

Plates displayed on walls usually need to be hung with the aid of a plate wire which clips around the back of the plate and onto the front by means of four sprung hooks. The plastic-coated variety are best because they reduce the possibility of chipping or rubbing the gold band on a rim. There are several ways to hang a plate collection. You can place a plain panel of wallpaper, paint or material on the wall as a backgound. Wallpaper panels can look very attractive when framed with a contrasting paper border. Fabric panels can be either stuck directly onto the wall and edged with a strip of braid or thick ribbon, or stretched over a piece of chipboard or cork which in turn can be hung on the wall. Before hanging your plates it is best to work out the formation or shape you wish to achieve on a table top. Once you have decided on the design, then hammer the hooks into the wall, making sure that the spacing is accurate and the order is correct.

Good lighting is important to achieve the maximum impact from your display. Poor lighting can dull and detract from even the most charming arrangement. If your arrangment of china has a permanent home you could install small spotlights or down-lighters to pick out certain special pieces. The type of light bulb you use will also have an effect on the overall appearance. Some fluorescent bulbs give a blue tint, other bulbs have a yellow cast. Tungsten halogen bulbs give a good white light which shows up colour accurately but it may be helpful to discuss the type of bulb suitable for your purpose with the staff of a reputable lighting shop.

Lighting in a display case or cabinet is particularly important, small spotlights should be angled and adjusted to highlight the figures inside the case. There is little enjoyment to be had from a lovely collection that you can't see in the gloom of the cupboard or hidden by the reflection on the glass of the doors. However, care must be taken to ensure adequate ventilation or dispersal of the heat caused by light bulbs.

CARING FOR YOUR ROYAL DOULTON COLLECTION

Over the years I have been amazed by the way people handle some rare and delicate pieces of Royal Doulton. On a trip to New Zealand in 1991 we were having an evening cocktail party in a store when a person came in with a huge brown paper garbage bag (plastic bags are not allowed in New Zealand for environmental reasons). From this paper bag the visitor produced one of the most stunning Burslem vases I have ever seen. The piece should certainly have been in some important museum instead of being carted around in a vulnerable paper bag. In a store in Nova Scotia, Canada, a lady came up to me with a huge basket – she proceeded to unravel her collection of figures from a mass of pantyhose that she had used to wrap them in. Another surprising arrival in a department store in Canada was a man with his Royal Doulton lavatory – a lovely example of a very early lavatory decorated with a dense, blue floral design. He said he put cut flowers in it at home!

CLEANING

Most items, apart from dishwasher-safe tableware, should be done by hand. Depending on the type of glaze or finish there are a number of different ways of cleaning.

Underglaze china is so called because the colour or decoration is sealed and protected by a final, top layer of glaze. Underglaze decoration is often more vivid in colour because the pigment has been applied straight to the biscuit-fired surface rather than onto an already glazed surface. Character jugs often have an underglazed face, the mottled, realistic colouring is achieved by painting the textured biscuit surface. Some figures and animal models are also decorated underglaze.

Wash underglaze china gently in hand-hot water (no more than 60°C) with a solution of washing-up liquid or detergent (one teaspoon to a pint of water). Never use very hot water as this can cause crazing or cracking of the glaze. Use a plastic washing-up bowl and put rubber guards on the ends of the taps to avoid chipping your china should you knock against the hard metal. Rinse each item with warm clean water and drain on a plastic draining mat. Polish with a fluff-free soft cloth. Do not immerse metal-mounted, or capped pieces in water as it may encourage the metal to rust and this will stain the ceramic. Always clean metal and ceramics separately.

On-glaze china is glazed first then decorated and fired again, but the colour is closer to the surface of the china and is therefore more vulnerable. To clean on-glaze areas it is advisable to ask your local drug store or chemist for a non-ionic detergent (non-ionic detergents do not dissolve or lift the colour during cleaning). If non-ionic detergent is not easily available, use acetone or methylated spirits, which should be applied gently with a cotton wool ball or swab.

Boy on a Crocodile (HN373, Charles Noke, 1920–1938).

Images figures displayed on perspex blocks to form an attractive group. Left to right: Brothers (HN3191, Eric Griffiths, introduced in 1991); Happy Anniversary (HN3254, Douglas Tootle, 1989-1993); Bridesmaid (HN3280, Robert Tabbenor, introduced in 1991); and Over The Threshold (HN3274, introduced in 1989).

Character jugs can be displayed and used throughout the home; they make attractive additions to the bathroom.

For cleaning and care of Royal Doulton figures we would recommend that extremes in temperature or rapid changes of temperature are avoided. Figures should be washed individually in a plastic bowl in a luke warm solution of mild hand-wash detergents, using a soft artist's paint brush. Care should be taken to seal the hole in the base of the figure prior to washing to prevent water getting inside the figure. Figures should then be gently dried with a soft cloth and allowed to air dry before placing on display.

PROTECTING YOUR CHINA

Keeping your display behind glass in a cupboard or display case will protect it from dust and general household grime. This type of protection will also cut down on the necessity for frequent cleaning.

If there are cigarette, pipe or cigar smokers or a smoky fireplace in the room where your collection is housed, periodic wiping with acetone or methylated spirits will remove the accumulated nicotine or soot residue. Glass shelves in this sort of environment will also require regular cleaning.

If possible, use perspex or wooden rather than glass shelves. Frequent contact with glass shelves often results in small but numerous chips to the base of ceramic objects. If you do have glass shelves try and take extra care when lifting and replacing china objects.

Small display labels can be informative and a useful record of when and where a piece was bought or given. Labels should not be stuck onto on-glaze china or gilding as their removal may cause damage. Small pieces of white postcard or even decorative cards used for table place settings can be bought from a local stationery shop and set at the foot or side of the piece to which it relates.

Insurance and Valuation: Try to keep an up-to-date photographic record of your collection for insurance purposes. An additional benefit of this precaution is that in case of an accident a professional restorer will find accurate photographs a great help in his repair work. On the back of

Limited edition figures depicting portraits of the Royal Family can be found in the Sir Henry Doulton Gallery, left to right: Duke of Edinburgh (HN2386, Peggy Davies, 1981), Queen Elizabeth The Queen Mother (HN3189, Eric Griffiths, 1990), Queen Elizabeth II (HN2502, Peggy Davies, 1973) and The Prince of Wales (HN2884, Eric Griffiths, 1981)

each photograph make a note of the date of purchase or when you received it if it was a gift. Add the price if you know it or an estimate if possible. Also note any marks on the base of the pieces and record any distinctive features. All this information is useful for an insurance assessor and in helping to identify a piece should it be lost.

SIMPLE RESTORATION

If you collect rare or old pieces you will often come across items that are a little damaged, and if you are looking for a missing figure to complete a collection you may be forced to fill the gap with a less-than-perfect specimen. You may also be unfortunate enough to break a treasured piece in your collection and find that a simple repair will restore it to former glory.

The golden rule of restoration is that any repair you carry out must be fully reversible so that no further damage or staining is incurred. If you are in any doubt about tackling a simple restoration, particularly if the piece is valuable to you, then you should take it to a professional china restorer.

Broken glazed pottery will show two distinct layers, the porous, white body and a glazed, glass-like layer on the outside. It is important to keep all or as many bits of broken pottery as you can, as each tiny chip can be glued back and will help to achieve an effective repair. Make sure each piece of pottery or china is thoroughly clean before embarking on the repair.

If you buy a piece that has already been repaired once it is likely that old unsightly adhesives will have to be removed, the piece dismantled, thoroughly cleaned, then reassembled and glued. It is helpful if you can identify the type of glue

that has been used to make a previous mend, but if you cannot it is a matter of trial and error until you find the method that breaks the bond. Glues based on animal products are quite common and will eventually break down by soaking in warm to hot water. The best approach is to submerge the piece of china in lukewarm water then increase the temperature of the water gradually. When the glue has softened the parts can be gently pulled apart. Cellulose adhesives such as Durofix will break down with acetone or nail varnish remover applied with cotton-wool swabs. Epoxy resins such as Araldite and Shellac, and rubber solutions such as Evo-stick can all be removed by using Nitromors paint stripper. When using Nitromors on an absorbent body such as earthenware, the object should be pre-soaked in water. The stripper, applied along the joint, will eventually eat down into the old adhesive and the joint will part. Repeated application may be necessary for a stubborn or old join.

After the object has been dismantled, any surplus adhesive should be carefully removed with a sharp blade or with repeated washing with paint stripper. All break edges then have to be cleaned using one of the previous methods. Never use household bleach to clean the pottery or china as it will clean the surface but may also remove glaze and colour. A mild solution of baby bottle sterilizing fluid will clean as effectively but without damage.

Leave the object to dry throroughly – this can take seven to ten days in the case of porous earthenwares such as terracotta. The smallest piece of glaze, old adhesive or dirt will prevent a perfect bond. A trial run of assembling the pieces without adhesive is a good idea so that you feel confident when it comes to making the final fitting.

The choice of adhesive is important. Epoxy resins should be avoided if possible as they are not easy to break down once bonded. These adhesives are best left to the experts. Some of the more recent developments such as the ten-second impact glues are generally not suitable either. PVA such as Evo-stick is a strong and a fast setting adhesive which is easy to use. Cellulose nitrate adhesives such as Durofix or UHU are easy to apply and can easily be removed with acetone. Before final bonding, check all the edges and make sure that your hands are clean. Apply the adhesive in accordance with the instructions on the tube and build up the object until all the pieces are fitted into place. You can wipe away any excess glue while it is still wet with a little lighter fluid or acetone on a cotton swab. Hold the pieces together with Sellotape or masking tape, squeezing any surplus adhesive from the joins. After twenty-four hours remove the tape – any residue adhesive from the tape can be simply removed with a little white spirit and a tissue.

Chips or missing pieces can be modelled with an epoxy resin filler such as Sylmasta, which is available from most artists' suppliers. Make the new part slightly thicker than the original, to allow for shrinkage during drying and leaving a little extra to be rubbed down with glass paper, to achieve an exact match in size and shape. This sort of repair can be painted to match the main piece, with acrylic paints and then varnished with a clear polyurethane lacquer.

ROYAL DOULTON ARCHIVES

Royal Doulton is fortunate in having comprehensive archives relating to both itself and many of the other Companies it now owns. The archives include pattern books, brochures, photographs, notebooks and newscuttings and are essential in researching the history of the company. When answering queries from collectors the Museum Manager Valerie Baynton and her team use them to verify information. Valerie and other staff also collect and document current information for future reference. Copies of all brochures and price lists are among the material retained. In the archives there are also examples of most pieces produced by Royal Doulton. An example of all figures, Character Jugs, a place setting from each tableware design and a selection of special commissions are all stored on rows of shelves – like a reference library but with china objects instead of books.

THE SIR HENRY DOULTON GALLERY

Since its opening in 1982 many visitors and collectors have made the Gallery the focal point of their visit. Her Royal Highness The Princess of Wales was a guest in 1984, and during her visit she was particularly taken by the collection of miniatures, and amused by the Virago inkwell. The inkwell depicts a squat, fierce-looking woman with her hair bound back in a scarf and her arms folded formidably across her waist. The words 'Votes for Women' are embossed on her apron and the head tilts back unexpectedly to reveal the inkwell.

American visitors have included Maureen Reagan who came to view the Character Jug of her father. The commander of the space shuttle *Discovery,* Commander Henry Hartsfield, presented the Gallery with one of the three Royal Doulton plates which achieved the accolade of being 'the first china in space'. Other visitors have included ambassadors, civic dignitaries, MPs and TV personalities. Collectors and first-time visitors to the factory in Burslem also find it a fascinating journey through the history and output of the Company.

The Gallery holds a large variety of Royal Doulton ware ranging from the early utility ware made at Lambeth in the 1820s and 1830s to the latest Pretty Ladies and my own Michael Doulton figures. Some rare and unique items are also on show, so it is a place to view pieces that cannot be seen elsewhere. The first showcase holds Lambeth Wares including an early spirit flask and a range of the Lambeth Artwares including pieces by George Tinworth, Hannah Barlow and the last two artists to work at Lambeth before its closure in 1956, Agnete Hoy and Vera Huggins. In the next case is an eye-catching and colourful array of the Sung, Chang and Flambé glazes, developed by some of the most noted Doulton artists from the early days of the Burslem factory. Pieces designed by artists such as C. J. Noke, John Slater, Cuthbert Bailey, Harry Nixon and Fred Moore can all be seen. The exotic shapes and stunning glazes are quite a spectacle.

In contrast to all this vibrant colour is the next showcase where the delicate artistry of such magnificent painters as Percy Curnock and Robert Allen can be seen. The softer glazes and detailed painting of these items draws many visitors to stand and study for a considerable time. In front of this case is a spectacular large vase by Edward Raby; also on view is the splendid Dante vase which is a special feature of the Gallery.

The far wall of the Gallery is almost entirely devoted to figures, with over 300 models selected from our archives on show at any one time. They are often displayed to illustrate a theme, such as Bathing Beauties or A Flair for Fashion, which gives the visitor an opportunity to see the various trends and influences in dress and facial decoration through the years. Our rare and valuable collection includes such figures as the Boy on the Crocodile and Marquise Sylvestra. The Boy on the Crocodile (HN373) is a rather bizarre piece by Charles Noke made around 1920. It is part of a series which includes Child and Crab (HN32) and Boy on Pig (HN1369). It is thought that the inspiration for these figures may have come from Charles Kingsley's *Water Babies* stories or perhaps Rudyard Kipling's *Jungle Book* tales. Both Boy on Crocodile and Boy on Pig were also produced in Flambé.

Marquise Sylvestra is an eye-catching model. The figure appears to be curtseying in an ornate eighteenth-century panniered dress. The skirts and bodice of the frock are elaborately decorated with gilded flower motifs and a fanciful blue edging. The Marquise covers her face with a tall mask which finishes in a hat-like model. The Marquise is rare because she has no HN number and is not thought to have been put into general production. The design is believed to have been inspired by Leon Baskt's design for a costume in a Russian ballet *The Good Humoured Ladies.* The role of the Marquise was danced in London by Josephine Cecchette who was an instructor with the *corps de ballet* in the 1920s. A model of the Marquise's partner, the Mendicant Fiddler, has yet to be discovered, he is known as an illustration in the pattern books in our archive collection.

It seems that there might have been a Fiddler figure because a newscutting from the *Musical Standard* of 21 February 1923 names this as one of a series of figures from the ballet *The Good Humoured Ladies* and it states that the figures were sold for seven guineas at Heals shop in London's Tottenham Court Road.

The next section of the Gallery illustrates the diversity of production of the Burslem factory with examples of Rembrandt Ware, Series and Advertising Wares. From the dark rich lustre of the Rembrandt and Kingsware flasks, a number specially made for whisky companies such as Dewars, to the delicate floral shades of the model of the Lavender Flower Seller for Yardley. There is a small section with a selection of Commemorative Wares, including the *Discovery* space shuttle plate and the Toby Gillette Character Jug. There are also a number of items relating to

Eric Knowles, Director of Ceramics at Bonhams, on a visit to Royal Doulton with the Old Salt Character Jug.

our Royal Family including the basalt portrait busts of Prince Charles and Princess Anne.

The Royal Doulton story is brought right up-to-date in the Gallery as the entire collection of current figures and Character Jugs are also displayed. All tableware designs and giftware, such as Bunnykins can also be seen. The magnficient and striking verdis-gris coloured ceramic statue of 'The Marriage of Art and Industry' by Peggy Davies, gives you a single lasting vision and food for thought as you leave the Gallery. But Royal Doulton history can be seen outside the Gallery as well as within.

Due to the restrictions of space in the Gallery, only a selection of our vast archives can be shown at any one time. Pieces such as Royal Doulton's 150th anniversary vase, made in 1965, and based on the traditional bottle-shaped kiln and overprinted with a gold portrait of the founder and a frieze depicting the Company's contribution to ceramics for home, industry and technology, are only occasionally on show. One exhibit that is too big to be shown in the Gallery

is a 1930s stoneware chemical jar, donated by the Nuffield Manufacturing Company from Redhill in Surrey. The jar is 8 feet high and 15 feet round. Sir Henry Doulton is famous for throwing a similar jar, which held 300 gallons, in celebration of his 21st birthday in 1841.

We are constantly adding to and updating the collection. Through special funds the Curator of the Gallery, Katharine Ellis attends auctions such as those held by Phillips and pieces that are missing from our own collection or other items of particular interest are added. Other items are on loan or donated to the Gallery. Details of new additions and finds, as well as new exhibitions in the Gallery are regularly reported in the Collectors Club magazine. An appointment can be made with Katharine if a collector would like to discuss a particular piece or to view any specific item in the archive collection. Booking a visit is not necessary for the Gallery which is open Monday to Friday 9 to 12.45 and 1.30 to 4.30.

Gloria Hunniford broadcast her radio programme from the Minton factory of the Royal Doulton Company, pictured here with two young Royal Doulton collectors and a series ware plaque.

A visitor book is maintained and HRH The Princess of Wales is just one of many Royals who have signed the book.

FACTORY TOURS AND VISITS:
Because of demand, all tours should be booked in advance. Please telephone Sandra Baddeley on (0782) 575454 or write to Royal Doulton Ltd, Nile Street, Burslem, Stoke-on-Trent ST6 2AJ, to arrange a visit.
John Beswick, Gold Street, Longton, Stoke-on-Trent, (0782) 313041
Royal Doulton Crystal Ltd, Amblecote, Stourbridge, West Midlands, 0384 395281.
Royal Crown Derby, 194 Osmaston Road, Derby, DE3 8JZ, 0332 47051.

ROYAL DOULTON INTERNATIONAL COLLECTORS CLUB
As Honorary President of the Royal Doulton International Collectors Club I often attend dinners, meetings and events with our club members. There are many advantages of being a member of the Collectors Club. The colourful quarterly club magazine, *Gallery,* is posted to members. The magazine is full of news and informative articles as well as details and photographs of the exclusive Collectors Club offers. The offers of figures, plates and Character Jugs are offered only to club members and they are very special indeed

There are invitations to our many events and free tours of the Royal Doulton factory. The Club also offers its members access to a free historical enquiry service operated by Royal Doulton's own expert museum staff.

A wide range of specialist reference books on Royal Doulton wares such as Character Jugs, Loving Cups, Series Ware and Flambé, as well as videos and gift items are available to Club members.

Club Headquarters and UK Branch: Minton House, London Road, Stoke-on-Trent ST4 7QD, England.
USA Branch: Royal Doulton USA Inc, PO Box 6705, Somerset, NJ 08873, USA.
Australian Branch: Royal Doulton Australia Pty Ltd, PO Box 47, 17-23 Merriwa Street, Gordon, NSW 2072, Australia.
Canadian Branch: Royal Doulton Canada Ltd, 850 Progress Avenue, Scarborough, Ontario M1H 3C4, Canada.
New Zealand Branch: PO Box 2059, Auckland, New Zealand.

For any enquiries for other countries, contact the Club Headquarters in Stoke-on-Trent.

Designs from the Figure Pattern Book showing Dunce (HN6), and Pedlar Wolf (HN7), both modelled by Charles Noke. Note the decorating instructions for each figure.

Bibliography

Eyles, Desmond, *The Doulton Lambeth Wares,* Hutchinson, 1975.
   The Doulton Burslem Wares, Barrie & Jenkins, 1980.
Eyles, Desmond, Baynton, Valerie, Louise Irvine, *Royal Doulton Figures,* Royal Doulton and Richard Dennis, due December 1993.
Gosse, Edmund, *Sir Henry Doulton – The Man of Business as a Man of Imagination,* ed. Desmond Eyles, Hutchinson, 1970.
Lukins, J., *Collecting Doulton Animals,* Venta Books, 1990.
   Doulton Flambé Animals, MPE.
   Doulton Burslem Advertising Wares, Venta Books, 1985.
   Collecting Royal Doulton Character & Toby Jugs, Venta Books.

Doulton Lambeth Advertising Wares, Venta Books, 1990
   Collecting Doulton Kingsware, Venta Books, 1992.
Irvine, Louise, *Royal Doulton Series Ware Volumes, 1,2,3 and 4* Richard Dennis, 1980-1988.
   Royal Doulton Bunnykins Collectors Guide, Richard Dennis, 1993.
   Royal Doulton Bunnykins Figures, UK International Ceramics Ltd, 1992.
   Limited Edition Loving Cups and Jugs, Richard Dennis, 1981.
Royal Doulton *Dating Doulton, A Brief Guide,* Royal Doulton Ltd., 1984.

Index